The
Basics
of
Supervisory
Management

The
Basics
of
Supervisory
Management

MASTERING THE ART OF EFFECTIVE SUPERVISION

James Menzies Black

College of Business Administration
University of South Carolina

McGRAW-HILL BOOK COMPANY

New York   St. Louis   San Francisco   Auckland   Düsseldorf
Johannesburg   Kuala Lumpur   London   Mexico   Montreal
New Delhi   Panama   Paris   São Paulo   Singapore
Sydney   Tokyo   Toronto

Library of Congress Cataloging in Publication Data

Black, James Menzies.
The basics of supervisory management.

1. Supervision of employees. I. Title.
HF5549.B55 658.3'02 74-26577
ISBN 0-07-005513-0

34567890 BPBP 7843210987

*The editors for this book were W. Hodson Mogan and Margaret Lamb,
the designer was Naomi Auerbach, and the production supervisor
was George Oechsner. It was set in Electra by
Monotoype Composition Co., Inc.*

Printed and bound by The Book Press.

To M. Joseph Dooher—A superb editor and a close friend whose patience, encouragement, and sound advice have helped me so much in writing this and other books.

Contents

The Supervisor and the Administration of Discipline. Signs of Disciplinary Troubles: Absenteeism; Tardiness. Insubordination. Illegal Work Stoppages. Conclusion.

Preface

The Basics of Supervisory Management can be used for different purposes by all levels of management. Its immediate audience is the working supervisor who serves as the connecting link between higher management and the rank-and-file employee. For him it is a short, to-the-point handbook that explains: how to analyze the assignment, how to make the difficult attitudinal adjustment that must be accomplished to complete the transition from "doer" (employee) to director (manager), how and when to use a variety of methods and techniques that are being utilized in the positive management of people.

Both line and staff executives will find much of value in this book. Staff people can adapt its material to supervisory training courses, or use the book itself as text for such programs. Department heads and operating managers above the rank of first-line supervisor will discover that the many checklists and guides are pertinent to their assignments and helpful to them in organizing their thinking. By reading the book as a "refresher" they can improve their planning and general administration of subordinates and thus upgrade their overall performances.

The Basics of Supervisory Management will also be helpful to the top management executive. From it he will gain fresh insight into the many complicated problems that the modern supervisor is expected to handle and receive an updating review on programs, methods, and techniques that have been successfully applied in the solution of these problems. Since the effectiveness of a company's supervisory training program depends so much on the degree of support it gets from top management, I hope this book will impress on high level executives the importance of such training and the imperative need to give company training programs solid and constructive support.

The book will also furnish the aspirant supervisor with an easy-to-read, easy-to-understand introduction to the responsibilities of the supervisory job together with clear explanations of the day-to-day problems supervisors face and how they go about solving them.

Lastly, The Basics of Supervisory Management may advantageously be used by junior colleges, by trade or technical schools, or by companies as a text for pre-supervisory training classes. Its chapters review the supervisor's management assignment in its entirety, and a student receives comprehensive explanations of what supervisors do, how they do it, what their problems are, and what both higher managers and employees expect of first-line supervisors in the performance of their duties.

In writing The Basics of Supervisory Management, I have tried to provide the reader with a concise summing up of the key elements of a front-line manager's most important job—getting things done through people. In earlier books on supervisory subjects such as *Front-line Management* and *The Front-line Manager's Problem-Solver* I have covered topics that, perforce, I am again discussing in these pages. However, here the treatment of subject is "different." In *The Basics of Supervisory Management* my purpose is to give all ranks of management a brief but fact-packed guide that encapsulates the principles of good supervisory management, and to implement and illustrate these principles with appropriate checklists, guides, recommendations, and illustrations.

I have always believed that the quality of trained supervisory and management leadership determines a company's productivity, the morale of its employees, and the ability of the organization itself to compete. While in some quarters today it may not be fashionable to emphasize the importance of personal leadership, survey after survey shows that certain supervisors are simply more effective than others in getting results from people and the reason is still job know-how plus leadership.

I recall a study published by the University of Michigan's Survey Research Center which pointed out that "the behavior of supervisors is a key factor in determining their groups' output." This study also reported that when its interviewers asked employees of high productivity supervisors the reasons for the effectiveness of their groups they gave credit to the leadership of their bosses and made such comments as: "He spends his time as a supervisor should—on scheduling, planning, training. He doesn't try to do our work"; "He respects us, he stands up for us, and he gives us recognition for good performance"; "He keeps his word and he keeps us informed"; "He's fair and he will listen to our side of an argument"; "If you have an honest complaint, he'll do something about it"; "He is top-notch in training, and he doesn't just train you for the job at hand but tries to develop your ability so you can be promoted."

The Basics of Supervisory Management throughout its pages emphasizes the importance of sound supervisory leadership and points up a fact that has been demonstrated time and time again —good supervision leads to high productivity while inferior supervision is a deterrent to output.

The author is not concerned with particular styles or personal methods of leadership. They change with times and circumstances and leadership methods vary with the individual. A system or approach that is used effectively by one company or person may not succeed if used by another. But regardless of method or system the example of practices of trained supervisory leaders who know how to evoke positive employee response to the attainment of their goals, who have learned how to gain and retain employee respect and support, have a worth beyond price to their companies. Therefore a major objective of this book is to provide a guide to supervisors on how to cope with their day-to-day problems and how to increase the effectiveness of their own programs of self-development as leaders.

"A good leader must be what he wants his subordinates to become," wrote General Sir William Slim, distinguished British soldier of World War II. Such advice may sound quaintly idealistic in this decade of cynicism. But whatever the type of system, good leadership and its example will always be the vital factor in the success of any group activity. Those who may disagree with this statement will see its truth if they will only stop to think—What happens to people when there is a lack of leadership or leadership is inferior? Yes, what happens to people? To institutions? To companies? To nations? For this reason, *The Basics of Supervisory Management* accents the essentiality of intelligent and positive supervision. Fundamentally, sound supervision is nothing more or less than good leadership in action.

James Menzies Black

ONE

How to Think Like a Manager

There is a difference between doing something yourself and telling somebody else what to do and how to do it. That difference is "management." The highly skilled, productive employee who is promoted to supervisor often finds this difference the most difficult obstacle he must overcome to become successful in his new job.

Why? Because the rules of the game for the manager are not the same as for the simple employee. No longer can he rely on his job ability, experience, and know-how. He must now depend on other people. Formerly his work was simple. The boss gave him an assignment, he decided the best way of doing it, and he began, answering only to his superior and himself for the finished result. Now he is being asked to change totally his mental approach to his responsibilities. Certainly he still has a boss and still gets orders, but now he is required to break down those orders into job assignments which must be delegated to employees he has selected and trained. His achievements are not measured in terms of personal accomplishment but by the accomplishments of his subordinates. His reputation stands or falls on how well he can train and direct other people to perform effectively as a group.

CHANGING OVER TO THE MANAGEMENT OUTLOOK

Many would-be managers find the task of directing subordinates frustrating and are unsuccessful. Highly competent themselves, they tend to disregard the fact that the job of supervision requires an altogether different process of thinking from that of simply being an employee. They make little or no attempt to learn the new skills or develop the new talents that their managerial position demands. Job knowledge, technical skill, and hard work, they think, are enough to pull them through. They regard employees as order-takers who are certain to make mistakes unless they are closely supervised. Training is an effort, and besides, it cuts into production time. Communications? "A worker should know that when he's not doing all right he'll hear from me, so what's to talk about?" The consequence of it all is that such a supervisor is not a manager at all but a disguised worker trying to get everybody's job done except his own, and in the process jeopardizing his chance of career success.

These comments are not intended to discount the need for job knowledge, but a manager must use such knowledge indirectly. His job knowledge must be imparted to the employees who are directly concerned with doing the work; a supervisor who steps in and takes over every time there is the least excuse for doing so is rejecting his management responsibility or perhaps does not even understand it.

Few if any supervisors will admit they do not understand the responsibilities of their position; in fact, they could probably give an accurate account of their job descriptions. A supervisor's job is simply a management job, and a manager is responsible for planning, directing, coordinating, and controlling the activities of a group of employees and guiding their combined efforts for the achievement of a mutually desired objective. So far as the description is concerned, it fits any executive or supervisor from president to newest foreman. Aside from policy setting, the only difference is in the degree of responsibility.

There is nothing complex or hard to understand about the definition of a management job, or indeed about the theory of management. But that is the trouble with theory. Its implementation is difficult.

A vice president of a major corporation remarked:

> I doubt if there is a single executive in industry who doesn't know what a manager is supposed to do. But many of them fail to put their knowledge into practice. We all say that the only way to get results is by delegation; by giving people responsibility. Yet many managers never learn how to delegate properly.
>
> We all say that an employee has the right to know how he is doing; that it is up to the boss to give him the training, advice and counsel he needs to correct his shortcomings. Yet many managers are vague and general in their appraisal of subordinates and too busy to do much about training.
>
> We all say communications is the key to organization efficiency. Yet many a manager is so wrapped up in the vocational aspects of his work that he hasn't got time to attend to communications.

MANAGERIAL VERSUS VOCATIONAL ASPECTS OF A JOB

William Oncken, a management consultant, pointed out that failure to manage is a supervisor's biggest danger, saying:

> The difference between a professional and an amateur in management may be explained quite simply. The amateur likes to do what he does well. The professional knows how to do and likes to do what needs to be done. The inability to think like a man-

ager has lessened or destroyed the effectiveness of many otherwise competent men. They devote themselves to the tasks they like and neglect the others. All too frequently the work they enjoy is not management work at all.*

The inability to make the right decisions on job priorities is a not uncommon failing, especially for new supervisors. Many do not make the grade because they become so involved in the technical or vocational parts of their work they simply lack the time to direct subordinates. This human fault is not too hard to understand. A person is always sure of himself when doing that at which he is competent. If he can persuade himself that the job he wants to do is the job that should be done, he has provided himself with an excellent excuse for not allowing anything or anybody to interfere with its completion.

A manager must learn to separate those duties which are directly related to the management of people from those which are not and to give the former priority. Broadly speaking, any responsibility that directly concerns planning, directing, coordinating, and controlling the work of subordinates is a basic management responsibility. That which does not fall into this classification may be defined as vocational.

Every manager is loaded down with vocational responsibilities. There are reports to write, memos, letters. There are telephone calls, visitors, meetings of various kinds which take up time. Certain nonmanagement responsibilities are extremely important. All of them must be fulfilled. But the professional manager understands that managing people is his first consideration, and he does not permit himself to waste unnecessary hours or effort on those parts of his job that interfere with his major duties.

The president of a large bank observed, "It's not that some executives don't know the right way to manage, it's just that they find reasonable excuses for doing something else."

* William Oncken, Briefing Session #8, The Management Center, University of South Carolina, Columbia, Nov. 12, 1969.

"Doing something else" instead of managing people is an easy habit to acquire. The company president who makes an important speech to an influential citizens' group about the need for labor legislation may be performing a vital duty, but he is not managing anybody. He's doing a public relations job. Nor is the plant superintendent managing when he inspects a new machine and talks to experts from engineering as to where it should be located. He's involved in a layout decision. The sales manager who calls on a customer and brings home a big order has rendered his company a service, but it has nothing to do with his primary job of organizing, directing, and coordinating the work of his department. He has gone back to being a salesman. The supervisor who concentrates on reports and paperwork, or who constantly finds himself lending a hand in an emergency situation, may be shouldering a heavy load of work but he is still failing as a manager. He is directing his efforts toward vocational or secondary assignments, perhaps because he feels more comfortable doing them.

Naturally executives and supervisors are required to perform many duties that are only indirectly related to their prime responsibility of managing. It is important for a company president to be a good spokesman for his organization. A plant superintendent should take a keen interest in layout and everything else that goes on in his operation. A sales manager would be remiss in his duties if he failed to maintain his contacts and his "feel" for the market that comes from calling on customers. And a supervisor who neglects his vocational tasks—such as paperwork and record keeping—or who allows his technical competence to become out of date will probably find himself in deep water. There are many demands on a manager's time, but that is the price of responsibility. Time is not the enemy anyhow. The danger lies in its poor allocation, in failure to think like a manager.

The boss who goes into his office and closes the door with orders to his secretary to "keep everybody out until I finish this report" has guaranteed his privacy from all persons except his superiors. He has also isolated himself from the activities of his department, and if something goes wrong he may not even hear about it until he emerges from his self-imposed seclusion. If the report is indeed of paramount significance, he may be perfectly right to give it priority attention. But if he is using it to get away from other activities that demand his attention and from questions that require decisions, he is rejecting his managerial responsibilities. And if he frequently isolates himself and tries to manage by remote control, he has little hope of succeeding in his assignment.

WHY SUPERVISORS FAIL

The boss who gives production a higher priority than people reveals that he has little interest in employees except as order-takers. This type of supervisor may be extremely competent from the standpoint of job knowledge, but he limits himself because he refuses to make full use of the talents of subordinates. He tends to supervise too closely and to move in and take over any job that is difficult or important, neglecting the whole operation by giving too much attention to one of its parts. Heavily burdened by his self-imposed assignment of trying to keep all operations in his own hands, his follow-up is of the over-the-shoulder kind which irritates subordinates, prevents them from developing, and tells them plainly that the boss has little confidence in their ability to work on their own.

Such an individual does not think like a manager. He probably regards his own management as "they" and hardly considers himself a part of it. He prefers doing to directing, and this limits his usefulness. He has rewritten his job description and views himself as a sort of straw boss or gang leader—not a manager at all. Such supervisors are not exceptional. Occasionally they predominate at a company.

A certain manufacturing firm was beset by labor relations problems. Top management blamed a "radical" union and there was much to support this point of view. Grievances flooded the industrial relations department and too many of them found their way to arbitration. Eventually the company hired a seasoned industrial relations executive to straighten out its affairs.

It did not take the new executive long to discover that the first trouble spot to be eliminated was the attitude of supervisors, who, according to the union agreement, were designated as the management representatives responsible for handling the first step of the grievance procedure. In reality this step had long since been eliminated. When a grievance occurred it was the practice for supervision to pass it up to the industrial relations department for a decision. This practice had to be corrected before progress could be made.

The industrial relations director ordered a study to be made of the types of grievances being filed and learned that the company was getting more than its share of the complaint of "supervisors doing the work of employees." A series of supervisory meetings were held and supervisors were encouraged to express their opinions on what could be done to improve the state of management-union relations. Eventually the reason for the frequency of the grievance about supervisors doing the work of employees became clear.

An old-timer explained:

> When one of these knuckleheads fouls up a job, it's quicker to do it yourself than to stand over him and tell him how to straighten out the mess. Sure, he might file a grievance. But then again he might not. If he does it's the headache of the industrial relations department, not mine. If they can't settle the complaint it might go to arbitration, but this takes months. And we might win the case anyhow. In the meantime, the job has been done and it's my job to get out the work.

The industrial relations director reported:

> My problem wasn't the union, it was the attitude of the supervisors. They didn't think of themselves as managers or identify themselves with the company. They believed they were middlemen responsible for transmitting orders from their bosses to the workers. Before we could move forward we had to change their thinking and transform them into real managers so they could assume their full responsibilities. Unfortunately, the attitude of "doing" not "directing" had become so ingrained in some of them they were never able to make the change.

THE ROAD TO FIRST-THINGS-FIRST MANAGEMENT

The degree to which a supervisor masters the art of delegation determines his real capacity to move upward to higher administrative positions. Yet some managers never wholly grasp this fundamental fact and continue to attempt to give personal attention to every detail of their jobs, to the detriment of their total responsibility. To determine whether or not you are really *managing* instead of trying to get the work done personally, you must first analyze your working methods. The answers to the following questions will tell you if you have become a *manager* or are still a competent employee endeavoring to "straw-boss" a group of workers.

1. Do you set practical objectives which employees understand and accept when you give them assignments?

2. Do you consider it important for each employee to receive recognition for both individual and group accomplishment because it builds pride in organization and pride in personal achievement?

3. Do you have a system in which progress is automatically measured and checked as work advances to preestablished goals? In other words, do you always know where you stand and how much remains to be done before you reach your objectives?

4. Do you advise your employees systematically of how they are doing and where extra training is needed to effect improvement?

5. Do your employees have a good understanding of company rules and policies and the reasons for them?

6. Do you base the organization of your department on all the jobs it includes or just on the abilities and skills of a few capable people who are carrying almost all the load?

7. Do you get good performance from everyone, or do you write off certain subordinates as going nowhere, neglect their training, and try to keep them busy and out of the way by giving them routine or unimportant tasks?

8. Do you criticize your own job performance, frequently analyzing it to identify deficiencies which can be corrected or improved?

The last item is highly important. Constructive self-analysis is the first step toward self-improvement. From your own experience you know that supervisors and executives who are generally considered the best at your company have set for themselves extremely high personal performance standards and continually strive to increase their job skills and professional competence. When your own job falls into its proper perspective it becomes much easier to redirect your methods of self-training and to systematically reduce the errors that you made when you were less experienced.

THE MANAGER'S JOB IS FOR THE FEW

Obtaining desired results by organizing and guiding the efforts of other people takes skill in both planning and leadership. How successful a supervisor will be in moving up in his company depends on his ability to expand his talents for directing subordinates. Therefore he should constantly seek to increase his effectiveness in using the tools of a manager—planning, organizing, directing, and follow-up—because the more people he supervises, the more important and complicated these functions become.

How large a unit a person can manage effectively depends on his capacity to think in terms of the knowledge and skills of other people. Supervisors who do a superb job of managing a small department where they can exercise immediate and personal leadership may fail miserably if promoted to a more demanding responsibility. Generals of army divisions who were masters of their parts of battlefields have lost their hard-won reputations when given entire armies to command.

Anthony Jay describes this kind of situation in his book, *Management and Machiavelli,** when he discusses the tenure of Frank Pace as chairman of the board of General Dynamics. Jay describes Pace as a trained lawyer who had never run a business before he took over General Dynamics, an organization of 106,000 employees in nine divisions, which Jay calls feudal baronies. Pace decided to leave the company's nine divisions alone and allow them to be directed by their own executives. Quickly he found that he was virtually a prisoner of his own subordinates. He had abdicated his role of leadership and considered himself a sort of chairman of the board presiding over the discussions of independent company presidents. General Dynamics lost $425 million between 1960 and 1962, the largest product loss a company had ever sustained.

Illustrations of managers who moved upward into positions they lacked the skill to handle are many, for such misplacement can occur at almost any level of an organization. The capable first-line supervisor may fail miserably as the head of a small department, and similarly an efficient department head may not make a go of it when he wins promotion to plant superintendent. Success depends on an individual's ability to develop on his immediate job and grow into a higher job.

Some people are emotionally and attitudinally unqualified for management at all. Brilliant they may be, and they may be highly skilled and knowledgeable in their craft, technology, or profession.

* *Management and Machiavelli: An Inquiry into the Politics of Corporate Life,* Holt, Rinehart and Winston, New York, 1967, pp. 37, 144.

But if they are unhappy working within the scope of an organization, if they cannot take the pressure that leadership imposes, they cause grave injury to themselves, to their companies, and to subordinates who look to them for leadership and get instead either a spokesman for the opposition or a "gang boss" who psychologically has never accepted his promotion.

No new supervisor accomplishes an immediate transition from rank-and-file employee to manager. New attitudes, broader understanding, and a totally different way of thinking about a job and its responsibilities are not part and parcel of a managerial promotion. These come through learning and by experience. The length of time it requires for a particular supervisor to adjust to his new duties and begin to apply the professional approach to them varies with the individual. But the speed of such an adjustment is proportionate to the quickness of his change to thinking of management as "we" instead of "they."

THE MANAGEMENT ATTITUDE

A knowledge of the basic principles of management (planning, directing, coordinating, following up, and communicating) is essential to a supervisor. But being knowledgeable is only half the battle. The trick is to put that knowledge into practice, and to some people this may present insurmountable obstacles.

A French instructor observed that a student can never really speak a language until he begins to think in it. A large French vocabulary, a firm grasp of grammar, and the ability to read the language as easily as you do English do not transform you into a fluent conversationalist so long as you must mentally translate everything you want to say from English into French before you say it and do the reverse when you try to answer a question. It is only when you think naturally and automatically in French that you are really comfortable speaking the language and that people are comfortable listening to you.

An impressive job title, high status, and important responsibility may be given to you by a company. But that is as far as it goes. You have to prove by performance that you deserve the authority of your position, and this you cannot fully do until you act and think like a manager.

The successful manager is a professional who takes pride in his competence, which he recognizes is based on the competence of people he has trained and directs. He is a leader who is well aware that his leadership responsibility separates him from subordinates even if formerly he was at their level, and even though he still counts some of them as close friends. Such a separation does not imply a conflict of interests. Rather a supervisor has different and broader responsibilities, which have given him new interests. He now must think in terms of a group made up of individuals, whereas as an employee he thought of himself as an individual who was a member of a group.

The attitude of an employee is self-centered and horizontal. He may be, and probably is, loyal to his organization. But, humanly, in times of stress he puts his own needs and those of his own group above those of the organization as a whole. A supervisor must think of the operation as a whole. The employee thinks of only his part of it. A supervisor must take into account the long-range consequence of his decisions. The employee is usually concerned with their immediate impact. A supervisor must be familiar with and always consider related operations in other departments when he makes plans. An employee may seldom give the associated workings a thought. Lastly, a supervisor's allegiance must be to the leadership of the organization because he himself is a member of that leadership, and if it loses the support and confidence of employees, the organization itself is endangered and everyone's job security and future are in jeopardy.

The fact that a manager is expected to carry out company decisions and administer company policies does not mean that all decisions and policies must be accepted blindly and without question. A supervisor has an obligation to himself and to his subordinates to present his point of view and to argue his position when he disagrees with a proposed course of action. However, when debate is concluded and a decision has been made, it then becomes his responsibility to implement that decision loyally and do his best to make it work, even if he disagrees with it. When you are a manager all decisions of management become your decisions, all policies of management—not just those of which you approve—are your policies.

A supervisor's loyalty to management does not indicate that his interests run counter to the interests of employees or that he is or should be in opposition to them. After all, he is their leader, and as such he owes them loyalty. To win their support he must defend their legitimate interests and provide them with the training, coaching, and counseling they require.

But leadership is a lonely job. A supervisor can be a friend of *all* of his subordinates, but not just of a few. He must also remember that the boss who attempts to curry favor with employees by trying to be "a member of the gang" is making a serious error.

WHAT IS YOUR MANAGEMENT ATTITUDE?

Candid replies to the following questions will help you see precisely how you think about your management job and whether you are thinking, acting, and feeling like a member of the management team.

1. Do you automatically sympathize with the employees when there is a conflict of interest or a dispute with management? Does your sympathy show?

2. Do you explain or justify it when employees criticize a company policy, decision, or action, or do you indicate by word or gesture that you also disagree but still must carry out your unpleasant enforcement duties?

3. Do you accept a company explanation about a new policy,

a decision, or an unpopular practice as sincere, or do you greet it with skepticism?

4. Do you reveal by voice, tone, facial expression, or manner that you are simply passing along higher management's orders and are in no way responsible when you give instructions of which you do disapprove?

5. Do you express your views to superiors and support them with reasoned and factual arguments when you think a policy or a decision is wrong or that it cannot be implemented properly, in this way trying to get things changed, or do you let management believe you agree, thereby playing a double game and using subtle methods to let subordinates know otherwise?

6. Do you take the blame, so far as your superiors are concerned, when an employee makes a mistake in your department, or do you try to escape responsibility by exposing the person responsible?

7. Do you resent managers and executives who have better jobs and suspect that they gained their positions through favoritism?

8. Do you take pride in your subordinates, being quick to defend them from the criticism of colleagues, recognizing their achievements, and pushing for their promotions, or do you subscribe to "Theory X" and think that most subordinates are loafers who will only do a fair day's work when you ride herd on them?

9. Do you play favorites among subordinates, or do you always try to give each one fair and consistent supervision?

10. Do you try to cover up poor group performance by attributing it to supposed delays or schedule breakdowns that occurred elsewhere, because you think your first loyalty is to your subordinates and not the organization as a whole?

11. Do you accept "get-by" work that is below minimum standards from certain employees you feel sorry for, although you know deepdown they will never become satisfactory?

12. Do you wink at tardiness, overlong coffee breaks, or early washups because you think such practice does not hurt much anyhow and it will earn you employee goodwill?

13. Do you give everybody high marks when you report to higher management on individual performance appraisal results because you think telling things like they are would make you an informer?

14. Do you let certain influential employees (for example, a union shop steward) get away with it when they break company rules, because you think it might lead to trouble if you took proper action?

15. Do you make "side-deals" or undercover arrangements with employee representatives that are partially or wholly inconsistent with company policies and practices?

16. Do you really prefer to do a job yourself instead of training someone else to do it?

17. Do you tell employees how they are doing in their work, or do you let them know you do not like to be bothered and if they are not doing well they will soon hear about it?

18. Do you have the attitude on communications of, "Obey the rules, don't argue about them," and "I'll tell you what I want you to know; anything else is none of your business"?

19. Do you delegate tightly and try to keep everything in your own hands by close follow-up because you do not trust subordinates and are afraid you will be blamed for their mistakes?

20. Do you really think of yourself as a member of the management organization?

WHAT MANAGEMENT AND EMPLOYEES EXPECT FROM A SUPERVISOR

Effective supervisors are in great demand by industry, and companies offer them many roads to advancement. When a person is made a supervisor, his company believes that he has, at least potentially, certain skills and characteristics which with further development will make him a valuable member of the management organization.

Milton M. Mandell and Pauline Duckworth, writing in *The Selection of Management Personnel*, list the factors industry thinks contribute to a supervisor's success. They are the result of a survey of 770 rating officials. This checklist, in descending order of frequency of response, may be of help to any supervisor who wants to evaluate his own strengths and weaknesses. A successful supervisor:

1. Has all-around knowledge of trade.
2. Cooperates when changes are needed.
3. Requires little supervision.
4. Is industrious, interested in work.
5. Meets deadlines.
6. Plans and organizes well.
7. Continually increases in trade knowledge.
8. Continually seeks improvements in methods.
9. Is respected by his men.
10. Keeps superior informed on work progress.
11. Trains men well.
12. Is honest and straightforward.
13. Has a sense of humor.*

Anyone reading this list would probably agree that item 13 is an absolute must. A supervisor who possessed all of the foregoing virtues would obviously be too good to be true. The attributes described are those of the "perfect" supervisor, and he has not yet made his appearance on anybody's payroll.

Nevertheless, the talents and qualities that authors Mandell and Duckworth have recorded provide a standard that every manager should try to reach. Considered separately they also tell much about the management job. Take the first item, "Has all-around knowledge of trade." This knowledge is the basis on which the manager must build his career. It underwrites his competence. If

---

* Milton M. Mandell and Pauline Duckworth, "An Objective Scrutiny of the Supervisor's Job," in Joseph Dooher and Elizabeth Marting (eds.), *Selection of Management Personnel*, American Management Association, New York, 1957, vol. I, pp. 89–90. Reprinted by permission of the publisher.

a supervisor's knowledge is inadequate, he cannot hope to carry out his job responsibilities. However, it should be noted that all other factors on the list have to do with his ability to achieve his objectives through the management of people.

Now that you know what management wants from a supervisor, do you wonder what the common faults are? Strangely enough, about the same thing, stated negatively. Mandell and Duckworth reported that supervisors held in the lowest esteem had the following faults, in descending order of frequency of response.

An unsuccessful supervisor:

1. Has insufficient trade knowledge.
2. Tends to be argumentative.
3. Is critical of change.
4. Is lax in discipline.
5. Lacks initiative.
6. Doesn't meet deadlines.
7. Does little training.
8. Lacks patience.
9. Becomes excitable and unnerved under stress.*

These lists add up to one fact. Both employees and higher management want supervisors who are managers in the full sense of that word, and the criticisms workers level at poor supervisors, like those of management, are based on the supervisors' failure to live up to their responsibilities. In short, both management and employees expect a supervisor to be a good leader, to be able to set objectives that he requires subordinates to attain, and to provide them with the training and the reasons for doing so.

CHARACTERISTICS OF A GOOD SUPERVISOR

From the foregoing and similar surveys we might sum up the characteristics that distinguish a competent supervisor as follows.

* Ibid., p. 89.

1. Technically he has a sound understanding of his job.

2. He is a good planner. Operating schedules are efficient, assignments are promptly made, and working time is utilized effectively.

3. He is a conscientious communicator. Employees always know how they stand with him and how they are doing on their jobs. He is willing to discuss work-related problems sympathetically and is receptive to new ideas. He listens to complaints and, if they are justified, he does something about them. Company policies and practices are explained, as are the reasons behind them.

4. He is a thorough trainer. The development of the skills and abilities of employees receives his top attention. A patient and careful instructor, he makes certain that workers, especially new ones, get the coaching they need to meet department standards.

5. He sets realistic standards and explains them. There is no confusion or uncertainty among employees as to what is accepted as good performance. Work standards are explained to make certain that subordinates know they are realistic and fair.

6. He is consistent. His methods of management are even-handed and objective. Employees know what to expect of him and have confidence in his judgment.

7. He is self-disciplined. He understands that disciplined leadership is the foundation of positive employee discipline. When crises happen, he keeps his head. He strives for objectivity and keeps a tight control over his temper.

8. He is available. He takes a sincere interest in each of his subordinates and knows their abilities and skills as well as their limitations. This knowledge helps him in delegation and in training. He is always willing to talk things over with workers and give advice and help on job problems. At the same time he never forgets he is a manager and not "one of the boys," so he does not make the mistake of trying to curry favor with subordinates by putting himself on their level.

The characteristics described above as important to supervisory or management success are the result of self-discipline. No supervisor began his career with all of these attributes; each had to develop them. A manager may have a brilliant mind and great talent as a communicator, and he may be well informed in his particular field. But that does not necessarily make him a good teacher, a good organizer, or even a good communicator. Such skills he must learn.

A new supervisor will make mistakes. Ambitious to succeed, he may set exceedingly high work standards and become convinced that employees are deliberately lying down on their jobs because they fail to meet them. He may be impatient in dealing with employee problems and discouraged when certain workers do not learn as quickly as he thinks they should. However, if he is aware of the qualities that he should develop, he will recognize his mistakes and profit by them.

THE RESPONSIBILITY OF DIRECTING

Supervising work means directing it. *Directing* is assigning jobs, providing instruction, giving training, and coaching and counseling individuals. It is also listening to and ironing out the job-related problems of employees and adjusting grievances. It is following up on work to check its progress against approaching deadlines. In short, effective supervision is simply another way of saying positive and disciplined leadership that is directed toward attaining predetermined objectives with quality results in a given length of time. The planning and organizing work of a supervisor is done before he can even begin to direct his subordinates properly. If planning has been sound and organization is efficient to manage subordinates skillfully, a supervisor still must:

1. *Give intelligent directions.* Directing is the "nuts and bolts" of the supervisory job. It is management in action, giving orders or

telling subordinates precisely what you want done. It is the suggestions and advice you offer to help workers perform effectively and the on-the-job training you provide to correct improper performance so that the task can be done more efficiently and easily.

2. *Provide advice and counsel.* It is to you that an employee instinctively turns when he needs help or wants to know how to improve his skills or develop his talents. He comes to you with problems, not all of them directly job-related. This provides you with an opportunity to get to know him and understand his problems and his ambitions. An experienced supervisor cultivates the art of listening and does his best to give help whenever possible or to steer the employee to experts when he cannot supply the need. Counseling is a built-in part of the leadership assignment. For any difficulty an employee has, whether or not it directly concerns his job, may adversely affect his efficiency, his morale, and his attitude, and if it is not solved, it can injure the organization as a whole.

3. *Motivate.* "Winning is everything," was the fiercely competitive challenge of the late Vince Lombardi, who knew that the best kind of coaching could not produce a winning football team unless the players were highly motivated. A leader in any competitive enterprise must build in his group the will to win and the conviction that it can. A result-getting supervisor must motivate employees to want to reach company objectives. This he does, not only by building their self-confidence, but also by winning their confidence in his leadership and in the organization. A highly motivated employee team enjoys competition, and its individual members are proud of the part each plays in the success of the team.

4. *Coach and train.* A supervisor sets employee performance standards and evaluates their work. But new people entering his department do not come already trained. Some of them may have special skills or experience in similar jobs elsewhere. But they must

still be instructed in your company's working methods and work standards. Training involves skill in various teaching methods (on-the-job counseling, group training etc.), and a supervisor must know how and when to use each. But all training is vocational. Its object is to help employees develop their skills and talents and increase their job knowledge. It takes constant work and care to be a good trainer. But the payoff is big. Aside from the satisfaction of developing highly competent subordinates, their efficient job performance reflects credit on you.

5. *Delegate.* When you became a supervisor, your company gave you the responsibility for managing certain resources, including men, money, material and machinery. You build your management reputation on the talent you demonstrate in getting the most out of these resources. By intelligent delegation you can enlarge your ability to accomplish results. *Delegation* means that you no longer perform a single job. You must plan, organize, and direct the work of many jobs. Delegation is the one action of a manager that separates the individual rank-and-file "doer" from the managing director of a group.

6. *Control.* A manager is responsible for the various activities under his direction. Every day new work is started and work in process is nearing completion or somewhere in between. The methods you develop to follow up and keep check on activities you direct are your controls. Controls enable you to measure progress and decide whether it is satisfactory or whether plans must be revised. An effective system of controls sounds a warning bell when operations get off the track, giving you time to take corrective action. Efficient controls make a supervisor's job easier. They permit him to make certain that each subordinate is moving forward satisfactorily, and they form the nervous system of management without which the manager could not coordinate many separate activities. They also are an alarm clock assisting him in the proper use of time. Finally, controls are valuable in judging one's own per-

formance. A good supervisor learns from mistakes and in the process acquires experience, on which good judgment is based. In the evaluation of your own management performance merely check your controls. They tell the story and let you know how you are measuring up.

PROFILE OF A PROFESSIONAL

The key to supervisory achievement is learning how to put first things first and thus acquiring a truly constructive management attitude.

Mentally the professional manager is thoroughly disciplined—so much so that many of his decisions are almost automatic. His firm technical grasp on his job and his clear knowledge of the objectives he wants to attain help him make decisions confidently. Nor does he back away from hard choices that he should rightfully decide simply because they are risky. He has accepted his management responsibilities, he is a member of the management team, and he knows that the quality of his leadership has an important bearing on company accomplishment. He is genuinely interested in the development of each of his subordinates and objectively fair in his treatment of all of them. At the same time he instinctively identifies himself with management—its policies are his policies, its decisions his decisions, its goals his goals.

It is true that on occasion he has differences of opinion with superiors and associates. When this occurs he expresses his views strongly and frankly. Sometimes when his arguments are persuasive his position is accepted. But whether or not his ideas prevail, when a course of action or a policy has been decided he does his best to carry it out successfully.

But the make-or-break test of a supervisor's is the competence, initiative, and productivity of his working team. If he cannot provide the leadership, direction, and training necessary to mold the talents and abilities of a collection of individuals into a cooperative organization unit, he will not win managerial success regardless of his intelligence, technical knowledge, or willingness to work.

Finally, the professional manager never forgets that the extent of his achievements depends on the willing support he receives from subordinates. The supervisor who is concerned about employees and available to them usually builds greater group efficiency than does his associate who is almost totally preoccupied with production. The so-called "people-centered" supervisor has learned to think like a manager.

TWO

How to Plan Your Work Effectively

To master a management job you must be able to plan effectively. Your ability to organize the activities of employees, to direct and control their work, to coordinate their various assignments, and to combine them into a cohesive whole depends on your ability to plan.

Think of it this way. A sound plan of action and the effective implementation of that plan are the bridge across which an idea travels from your brain to final accomplishment. An idea is useless until you have planned how to make it a fact.

Efficient planning also allows you to handle several operations simultaneously and give proper attention to each. It assures the logical development and orderly progress of your programs and guards against uncoordinated actions that cause imbalance in your supervisory methods. So, as a plant manager told a group of new supervisors, "The first step in learning your management job is to learn how to plan it. That way you can put everything together. If you don't learn how to plan, no matter how hard you work you will be backed in a corner by problems largely created by yourself. The line from the song, 'Wishing will make it so,' is very pretty. But you won't get anywhere by wishing. You must learn how to plan."

THE SUPERVISOR'S PLANNING RESPONSIBILITY

The planning duties of rank-and-file personnel are directed at how to do a particular job; those employees do not have to make plans for others. The supervisor, on the other hand, has a very different and much more complex planning assignment. When he plans his own work he must automatically plan the work of subordinates. Who is to do what? How? And by what time? Before the supervisor can plan properly he must learn the trick of split-level thinking, that is, thinking broadly and in detail. He must have a precise understanding of the overall objectives and be able to break down the whole of his assignment into its parts, decide on the relative importance of each, and delegate the separate parts to employees qualified to perform them.

The supervisor accomplishes his work by the skillful management of subordinates. People, not things, are his first concern. Therefore he must know how to plan and organize the work of people to secure a desired result. The better he is at utilizing their skills and talents and at coordinating their activities, the better he is as a manager. This means he must develop an ability to analyze and interpret information intelligently or his operation will sputter like an ancient automobile engine on a cold morning or it will fall apart completely. You are lost if you depend on "muddle-through" methods which allow you no control systems to keep you on top of your job and to warn you of danger spots. By strenuous effort, including doing the work of subordinates, constant troubleshooting, and good luck, you may be able to cope with the routine which you are forced to handle like an emergency. But real problems are certain to pin you to the wall and set you up as a target for the unexpected.

The effective supervisor has learned that a carefully worked-out plan of action is his road map to tomorrow, and he thinks of his job as a continually unfolding series of assignments in which one program's termination must blend with the beginning of another smoothly and easily. The boss who has the attitude, "Tomorrow's another day. I'll think about its problems when they happen," is making sure they will happen. Not only does he have fresh problems on every tomorrow, but he usually carries over into each morning a heavy packet of yesterday's troubles that still must be handled. Worst of all, he never has time to plan, and so he must come up with all of his solutions "off the cuff."

Some obvious signs of poor supervisory planning are: idle employees waiting for orders; uncertain employees not quite sure of what is expected of them, who perform unnecessary tasks, duplicate the work of others, or do nothing at all. Accompanying such breakdowns in employee efficiency are symptoms of departmental ineffectiveness: for example, bottlenecks in scheduling, uneven workloads, failure of needed material to arrive, poor machine maintenance, and the like.

Poor planning has an immediate effect on employee morale. Workers have little confidence in a boss's judgment or trust in his decisions if it becomes apparent to them that he does not know what he is doing. Subordinates expect job competence in a leader, and they become resentful and indifferent when it is lacking. Cooperation cannot exist in a climate produced by indecisive supervision. Grievances increase, absenteeism and tardiness climb, productivity plummets, and quality standards are seldom more than minimally met.

A competent young stenographer who quit her job because her boss was a poor manager said during the exit interview, "The salary is good, and I liked working here until I got my present supervisor. He's driving me up the wall. He doesn't make any attempt to plan our jobs or to divide assignments fairly. Two or three of us get all hard jobs while the other girls do routine stuff or sit around reading magazines. I don't mind doing my share, and I like to keep busy, but I don't like to be imposed upon. Who wants to pound at a typewriter all day when everybody else is gossiping by the water cooler?"

THE ELEMENTS OF GOOD PLANNING

Your ability to plan well is underpinned by four qualities:

1. You must have a firm knowledge of your job, or your plans will go haywire because they are faultily structured and not based on technical know-how.

2. You must leave yourself a margin for error and not plan too-tight deadlines, or you will find yourself short of time if unexpected problems occur or if there are delays of some sort which slow you down.

3. You must know your manpower resources and make certain that your plan is practical from the standpoint of the abilities and skills of your people.

4. You must plan flexibly so that you have room to improvise or make minor changes in your plan without distorting the plan itself or affecting the final outcome.

A hard look at the elements of good planning shows how practical they are. Obviously you must have a technical knowledge of your job to do it properly. Even the newest supervisor should be aware of the danger of basing a program on inadequate information and starting out half-cocked to execute an assignment. Nor does it take long for hard experience to teach you that few plans are perfect—that things seldom go absolutely according to plan. So it is simply common sense to allow yourself "sidewise" running room which permits you to take corrective action to eliminate mistakes in your original planning if necessary. Furthermore, the best plan will fail if the people assigned to carry it out lack the experience, talent, skill, or will to do so. Finally, if you plan so rigidly that you can only be successful if everything functions at top efficiency, more often than not you will find yourself blocked off from accomplishment by your own false optimism and so securely bound to a demanding schedule that you are unable to make any changes in it withóut upsetting everything—and without being forced to begin all over again.

WHO WILL DO WHAT AND WHEN?

It matters not whether a job is difficult or easy; it is still up to the supervisor to say who will do what and by what time, and this demands of him special managerial traits. They are:

1. *A supervisor must have clear foresight.* An experienced manager knows the danger of improvisation. Prior to giving instructions he forms a clear picture in his own mind of exactly what he wants done so that he is in a position to issue clear, intelligent orders. The manager who depends on improvisation and "plays it by ear" is usually troubled by inefficiencies resulting from backtracking, duplication of work, confusion on instruction, and missed deadlines.

2. *A supervisor must be an effective organizer.* Organization is the key to group accomplishment, the machinery which permits individuals to blend their talents and skills and to work together cooperatively. When a goal has been set, the boss must decide what work must be done to reach it, and who has the skills and experience necessary for it. He knows how to make work assignments efficiently because he is fully familiar with the skills, initiative, and experience of each of his subordinates.

3. *A supervisor must establish standards of performance.* Nobody likes to work in the dark. Every subordinate has the right to know the standard of performance. He must meet that standard,

and therefore he must be given the time and the training necessary to measure up to it. In order for a performance standard to be meaningful an employee must understand and accept both the standard and the factors on which his performance is judged.

4. *A supervisor must establish the objective.* He must know where he is going, if he expects to have any followers. It is the job of the boss to set goals clearly, to satisfy himself that he has the resources, such as manpower, equipment, and material, to reach those goals, and to sell subordinates the idea that it is worthwhile to do so.

5. *A supervisor must develop and follow efficient procedures.* Procedure is the machinery which turns policy into practice; it is the chart that shows the most direct line to a given objective. The purpose of procedures is to guarantee efficiency in the accomplishment of results. If the procedures fail to meet this purpose, they should be revised or eliminated. A procedure is the means to an end, not the end itself. Some managers confuse the two and in doing so become hamstrung in red tape of their own manufacture.

6. *A supervisor must control costs.* A *budget* is simply an instrument of control which enables a manager to plan expenditures properly. A wise supervisor is cost-conscious, keeping close tabs on such potentially dollar-wasting items as absenteeism, tardiness, overtime, labor turnover, and scrap.

PEOPLE ARE THE KEY

People are the key to the success of any plan. A supervisor must base his programs on the personnel he has, not on employees he would like to have. He should also keep in mind that subordinates can make a boss look good and his plan a success even if it has "bugs" in it. But they can also cause a perfect plan to fail and a supervisor to fall flat on his face if they do not believe in the plan or trust his judgment.

But it is not a handicap to have to depend on your subordinates.

Who knows them better than you? You can even design your programs to benefit from the skills and compensate for the deficiencies of your people.

During the Revolutionary War, the tough frontier fighter Gen. John Morgan won a major victory over the British at Cowpens, South Carolina, because his battle plan was formulated not only on what he knew he could count on from his opponent, Gen. Banastre Tarleton, a cavalryman, but also on what he knew of the strengths and weaknesses of his own troops.

Morgan's forces consisted of a few hundred veterans plus a regiment of raw South Carolina militia. In a hard fight Morgan realized that though he could rely on his regulars, the militia would bid him a hasty farewell at the first sign of enemy hostility, and he used this weakness to his advantage.

The militia was stationed to the front of his own soldiers, who were carefully concealed in the woods and canebrakes surrounding the open field where the battle would be fought. One simple order was given to the militia: "When the British charge, fire your rifle, then head for home as fast as you can." This was an order the militia knew how to obey perfectly. They had executed the same movement in many previous engagements without even being asked to do so.

The battle began just as Morgan had anticipated. Tarleton, certain that he faced only frightened farm boys who would break and run at their first opportunity (they always had before), waved his sword contemptuously and his bugles sounded, "Charge!" The militia fired a single volley at the oncoming horsemen and quickly departed the field.

At this point Tarleton threw caution to the winds. Thinking the battle was all over except for the mopping-up exercise, he and his troopers had no chance when they were surprised, ambushed, and almost wiped out by Morgan's hidden sharpshooters. "They seemed to rise up out of nowhere," said one of Tarleton's survivors, explaining the defeat.

By intelligent planning based on the principle of making the best of what you have, the Battle of Cowpens is recorded as a major American victory that moved the Colonies a giant step closer to independence.

REALITY—THE TEST OF PLANNING

The danger inherent in all planning is making assumptions that are based on wishful thinking. A national publication* describes the misfortunes of the Fiat Company, which snapped up a Russian offer to build an $800 million automobile plant on a snow-covered plain near the Volga River. Fiat had promised to produce 500,000 cars a year for the automobile-hungry Russians, and prospects were bright for a profitable partnership of Western capitalism and Russian communism. But unexpected problems cost the company an extra $100 million, and Fiat, instead of earning a profit, was lucky to break even.

Here are some of the problems that were not contemplated when the original plan was designed. Russia had prescribed a tight three-year deadline, by which time Fiat had promised to have its cars rolling off the assembly line. But the Russian roads were so primitive that the chassis of the vehicle had to be redesigned to ride higher off the ground. Moreover, the company, finding that it could not buy quality parts and accessories from Russian manufacturers, had to build its own facilities to produce them. Forges and foundries were also needed. Fiat quickly discovered that Russia was far from being a worker's paradise, and some supervisors complained bitterly that their employees were a good bit less than "heroic." These employees were transported to and from work—a distance of about 7 miles— by bus, and it took an hour and a half to make the trip one way. As a result few employees

* *Time*, March 5, 1973, p. 60.

were ready to begin work before ten o'clock in the morning. But they made up for it by quitting a half-hour early to catch the home-bound bus. This meant that the company's working day was abbreviated.

Another Fiat criticism of Russian workers concerned "quality." A company engineer sadly commented that the Italian conception of maintenance was entirely unknown in Russia—a machine that had been leaking 40 pounds of oil a day for two weeks had not even been reported by its operators.

Finally Fiat overcame its difficulties and produced the automobiles. But the venture was virtually profitless. There were just too many unknowns to plan properly. Still, Fiat considered the undertaking worthwhile because it brought Russia into the machine age and gained valuable publicity and prestige for the company. More important, Fiat learned enough from the mistakes to profit elsewhere in Eastern Europe: Its planning for plants in Yugoslavia and Poland is much more realistic.

Reality is always a stern test of planning. What appears to be a perfect plan on paper may be a dud when you try to implement it.

WHY PLANS GO WRONG

There is no need to blame yourself when plans do not come off if the causes are circumstances beyond your control. You must simply pick up the pieces and begin again. But if it is even partly your fault, as in the Fiat Company's case, you can profit from the experience.

Sound planning is based on what is possible in a given situation. To make sure the same mistakes are not repeated, find the right answer to the question, "Why did the plan fail?" If you can determine the cause, you can do something about it next time.

Here are some reasons why plans go wrong.

1. *The supervisor was overoptimistic.* His high hopes, or per-

haps his desire to please his superior, persuaded him to implement a program based on highly unrealistic planning. He did not give the boss the facts, but told him what the boss wanted to hear. In such a situation objectives can be attained only if the supervisor gets maximum performance from people, machines, and equipment. His impossibly tight deadlines cannot be met if a single machine is idle for repair, if there is an unexpected schedule breakdown, or even if one of his employees is absent from the work group.

2. *The supervisor failed to check the facts.* He did not study the skills of the employees to whom he would delegate specific assignments, to make certain each was qualified. He did not consider the efficiency of machines and equipment and their state of maintenance. He did not look to see if there were any special situations—vacations coming up, holidays, other work of an emergency nature (especially in departments which must cooperate)— that would affect the program.

3. *The supervisor's communications was faulty.* No plan will work if communications is inadequate. A program cannot move forward smoothly unless everyone involved clearly understands the part he plays in its implementation. Too often supervisors who have given broad general instructions take it for granted that subordinates know exactly what is expected of them, but this may be far from the truth. As a consequence there are false starts, needless mistakes, and general confusion. Employees who vaguely understand their orders, associates in other departments counted on for cooperation who have not been given a proper explanation of what they are to do, superiors who have not been kept informed on progress, are all likely to make errors or take independent action that spells disaster for the most carefully thought-out plan. Trying to push forward a program without good communications is like driving a car that is missing on three cylinders. Communications—up, down, and crosswise—is a management must if you want to guarantee the success of a project.

FORMULA FOR SOUND CONTROLS

Controls are necessary for every management activity, for every program—simple or complex. The method of developing a system of controls is precisely the same whether you are planning a safety program or devising a plan for the extensive reorganization of your company.

To develop effective instruments of control you must think through these four steps:

1. Define your objective.
2. Set employee performance standards.
3. Decide how you will measure progress so you can take corrective action if necessary.
4. Establish deadlines.

The purpose of a control system is to help you check on work as it goes forward toward a preestablished goal. The entire process comprises three factors:

1. *An acceptable performance standard.* Subordinates must have a precise understanding of the performance standard to which they are required to measure up and must accept the standard as reasonable and fair. If employees believe a performance standard is unrealistic and inequitable, the entire control system will soon break down.

2. *An accurate method of comparing actual performance with the desired standard.* A supervisor must know where he stands in regard to the work for which he is responsible. Employees need the same information. They expect to be told if they are not meeting the boss's expectations and, if so, what they can do to correct the deficiency. A supervisor has many channels of information that keep him advised on the progress of the work—reports, personal inspection trips, and follow-up which includes talks with subordinates—and if the control system is functioning properly, he knows whether movement toward a desired objective is at a satisfactory forward speed; if it is not, he knows what to do about it.

3. *Corrective action.* A good system of controls quickly identifies planning errors and other difficulties that may cause a delayed deadline. When a control flashes a red light to the manager to tell him that a project is not proceeding according to schedule, he must take quick remedial measures. A person who is conscious of shortcomings or bad habits is better off than someone who is not. But if he makes no effort to correct them, his knowledge is of no value.

THE METHODS OF PLANNING

Just like a football coach, the alert manager knows that keeping control of the ball is vital to his success and that sound advance planning is the best assurance of ball possession. If your inability to develop a sound game plan forces you to act according to circumstances and not according to your own choice, you have lost control of your operation. The method by which you develop a sensible plan of action encompasses a step-by-step process based on five fundamental principles. They are:

1. *Establish the objective.* A classic example of unplanned action is the man who did not know where he wanted to go and so jumped on his horse and rode off in all directions. The leader who is all motion but no results seldom lasts long. So keep in mind that you cannot reach a goal until you have clearly identified it. When you have your sights squarely trained on the target, you will be able to see the obstacles that lie between and can decide how to eliminate or get around them. When this has been done you are ready to take planning step 2.

2. *Describe the project's framework.* Outline the limits within which your plan must be activated and make a list—at least a mental list—of the rules you will follow in executing it. Rules are like the protective rails along a mountain highway: they prevent you from running off the road if you come unexpectedly on a sharp curve. Rules in planning help you make sure your solutions

to problems are sensible and in line with your budget and the value of the objective you expect to achieve.

3. *Choose the right plan of action.* After you have set the goal and determined the rules, your next move is to select a course of action most appropriate to your needs. Here you have to consider such factors as time, money, manpower, material, other projects you are directing, and the importance of the objective itself. Always make certain your effort is worth its cost. If you accomplish your purpose but in doing so spend too much money, cause other programs to fail or be delayed, or use too much material, you will get little credit for your success. In fact, you will probably be blamed for bad judgment.

4. *Put the plan in action.* This is essentially a job in communications. It is smart management to "sell" employees the idea that the objective you have set is worth reaching. By doing so you encourage them to make suggestions that will help accomplish your purpose more easily and quickly. Employee participation in deciding on how best to implement a plan is the best way to win their support for it. The act of contributing their ideas and expressing their views gives workers a sense of proprietorship in the program and a feeling of accomplishment when it is successful.

5. *Follow-up.* Follow-up is necessary in every phase of management. It is especially important in the implementation of a plan. When you give the orders that start a project rolling, your job is just beginning. If you simply sit back and hope for the best, you endanger the success of the operation. Follow-up is the key to an effective control system. Reports, talks with employees, and visual inspection all enable you to check on progress and to make quick corrections in details of your original plan when necessary.

PLANNING TIME PAYS OFF IN INCREASED EFFICIENCY

A national management association suggests that every executive spend a good part of his time planning his work. Of that planning time, approximately 40 percent should be spent deciding how to handle immediate problems, 40 percent on next week's problems, 15 percent on problems a month away, and 5 percent on problems of the far future.

These figures are only a guide. But you can judge the effectiveness of your planning practices by comparing them with the above.

A supervisor who think that recommendations to devote a good share of his time to planning are exaggerated because he does not think he carries too heavy a responsibility for this phase of his work should take a closer look at his job. A plant manager tells the story of a newly appointed foreman who made such a mistake.

> He [the supervisor] worked hard, but his new position seemed too much for him. He couldn't get the hang of it. I called him in for a talk, and he told me, "Every time I get started on one job another job takes me away. I spend my time jumping from problem to problem. Before I can finish adjusting the set-up on a machine, somebody's after me about a tool that needs replacing, or an employee has finished an assignment and wants to know what to do next. It's running me crazy."
> I asked, "How much time do you spend planning?"
> "Planning?" he said in a puzzled voice. "I don't do any planning. That's your job."

This foreman could not have made a greater error. Even though you may have only six or seven employees reporting to you, you are in every sense of the word a full-time manager. First and foremost, you are accountable for the productivity of your people and must see that they get the most out of their working hours. So you must plan to avoid delays that add to cost and impair efficiency. Responsibility is also on your shoulders to make sure machines and equipment are in good working order and that needed material is available. You plan production schedules and determine how you can fit necessary training time into your busy schedule. Employees look to you for the enforcement of safety regulations and discipline rules. They come to you for the adjustment of complaints. You make job assignments each morning and must follow up on the various activities to make sure they are being performed properly. Finally, it is your responsibility to make certain that housekeeping standards are maintained.

You would have no chance of succeeding in accomplishing these many activities unless you gave considerable thought to planning your working day and allotting proper time to each responsibility. If you fail to plan wisely, the bill for your inefficiency is not a little one, nor does it take long for your superiors to become aware of your inadequacy. If equipment and machine maintenance is poor, if aisles are cluttered and unsafe, if quality is below standard, the signs are clear. The person in charge does not know how to manage.

Planning is a continuing responsibility of all managers and one that cannot be postponed. Charles B. Thornton, as president of Litton Industries, observed that sound planning was the foundation on which a manager built his career, and he added, "I have heard many ask, 'How can planning be done?' The word 'done' is incorrect. Any kind of planning is never done. It is a never-ending process, not a completed product."

HOW TO GET THE MOST OUT OF
WORKING HOURS

Time is a manager's most valued asset. The late Hiram Hall when vice president of Bigelow-Sanford Company said, "The manager who doesn't understand the importance of time and how to use it effectively can't really manage. Lost or wasted time can't be replaced. The supervisor who has trained himself to be master of his working day and not its servant owns the key to management success."

When a supervisor has solved the problem of job priorities and knows whether he is concentrating on the main task of "managing people" or doing something else, he will have greater skill in time control. Good time control enables him to give the right attention to each duty, just as delegation allows him to accomplish a number of individual jobs simultaneously. The inexperienced cook may understand how to cook certain specialties, but somehow he does not know how to cook a meal so all the dishes are ready at the same time. The real chef has planned the job. All the food is served piping hot when the dinner bell rings.

To make certain you are receiving full value for the working hours you are investing, the following suggestions may be useful:

1. *Plan carefully.* The manager who reacts to orders instead of acting on them is always racing the clock and needlessly wasting his time and that of employees by attempting to plan and perform simultaneously. Get ready for tomorrow's work today. The instructions will be logical and orderly and the flow of work even and sustained. It is irritating to subordinates to stand around idly each morning while the boss decides what everybody is supposed to do. Having equipment and material in the places needed minimizes the risk of schedule breakdowns or failure. So check your working methods and identify occasions when inadequate planning caused an expensive loss of time. A knowledge of past mistakes can prevent their recurrence.

2. *Cut down time waste by proper training.* Poorly trained employees take longer to do a job than do efficient workers and often do not do it as well. A well-coached subordinate understands what to do and how to do it. He does not have to be told what tools, material, or equipment he will need. A good manager begins a new subordinate's training program when he is assigned to him. Furthermore, each employee receives proper training when given a new or unfamiliar job and when a different method is substituted for an old one. The development of capable employees is a major responsibility, and the time spent in it is an investment in the full utilization of working time.

3. *Guard against loose organization.* Without organization, group activity is impossible. The purpose of organization is to keep managers and employees informed of who is responsible for

doing what. Efficient organization is characteristic of good management. It eliminates the time loss and duplication of work caused by overlapping responsibilities and by failure to assign certain responsibilities properly.

4. *Use time effectively.* The competitive supervisor constantly searches for better, more efficient means of getting the job done. Fully aware that time is his most valuable asset and that lost time is gone forever, he has developed great skill in making full use of it. He does not permit idle time to steal working minutes from working days and inculcates in his subordinates the knowledge that loose or slipshod working methods create gaps in coordinated organizational activities through which time slips away, draining maximum results from even the best employee effort.

5. *Start with the clock.* Keep a sharp eye on tardiness. Latecoming employees give time a head start and force you to play "catch-up" all day. Practically every company has a rule against not reporting to work on time, but too often managers fail to enforce it. If subordinates think you do not mind if they are a little late, soon you find that you are delayed every morning waiting for them to arrive for work.

6. *Watch absenteeism.* Absenteeism is expensive and always causes problems in the spread of workloads. When you are short of manpower, you cannot use time effectively. Make sure each employee understands the importance of his job and the contribution he makes to the team effort. The person who knows he is needed is not so likely to take unofficial days off. If an employee is beginning to make being AWOL a habit, talk to him and find out why. If this does not help, take stronger measures.

7. *Give instructions clearly.* Instructions which are given hastily or are not well thought out beforehand are likely to be incomplete, vague, or inaccurate and are an invitation to mistakes and lost time. The efficient supervisor plans his work assignments, their delegation, and his instructions when he plans the job—in advance. Employees know exactly what they are expected to do, when they are to start work, and when the job is to be finished.

8. *Use man-hours wisely.* Make job assignments based on the skill, experience, and initiative of employees. The object is to get the right number of people on each project. Too many employees on a job will force some of them to be spectators, and their time is not used effectively. Too few workers causes an uneven distribution of workload and increases the chances of mistakes and the neglect of details. Analyze the total task and separate it into its various parts. This help you decide priorities. Next make a similar analysis of manpower resources—men, machinery, material, and equipment. The information gained from such analyses enables you to complete each assignment in an orderly way with minimum lost motion and no duplication of effort.

9. *Emphasize safety.* Accidents are expensive in both time and money. The injured worker suffers physically and perhaps financially. You are deprived of his services and may have to spend time getting a replacement. It is good management to build good safety practices into employee work habits by helping employees understand that safety rules exist to protect them.

10. *Pay attention to housekeeping.* Efficiency is founded on order, and good housekeeping is a sure sign of the employee efficiency and motivation that come from effective leadership. On the other hand, a certain symptom of low morale, indifference, and wasteful working habits is below-standard housekeeping. Crowded aisles, improperly stacked shelves, and inadequate maintenance of storerooms cause time loss and cut into production. A good supervisor stresses good housekeeping in training programs and will not put up with anything less.

11. *Maintain good discipline.* An undisciplined work force cannot get results. It is the responsibility of a supervisor to administer discipline firmly and fairly, and failure to do so can often spell trouble. Good discipline is the safest insurance against time wasting and inferior working habits.

12. *Check on maintenance.* Having proper tools and equipment at the proper places and in the hands of the proper employees saves time. Conduct frequent inspections.

A SUPERVISOR'S GUIDE TO
SUCCESSFUL PLANNING

Compare your practice with the items listed below to discover how firmly your methods of planning are anchored to job knowledge, good judgment, and imagination. A plan must be developed in a logical, orderly manner, and it is of paramount importance that you have well-trained subordinates to make it a reality.

1. *Know your subordinates and study their abilities.* A successful manager knows the strengths and weaknesses of his people—their primary and secondary skills. Such knowledge helps him in delegation because he has learned how to use his "bench strength." He can fill in with somebody else when a key employee is absent.

2. *Maintain good records.* Good records provide information that helps you control individual and group productivity, costs, and waste. They tell you of performance history, absentee rates, costs, scheduling, and productivity levels of the past. From this you can find recurring problems and give special attention to them.

3. *Study manpower needs.* An alert supervisor is always conscious of upcoming employment needs. The installation of new machines, new techniques, or new methods means you will need to develop new employee skills or adapt old ones to new demands. Future manpower planning is necessary to keep a company competitive, and corporations like General Electric insist that managers at every level play their part in manpower planning.

4. *Keep fully informed on technological developments.* Changes that take place in your department have a direct bearing on the jobs of your subordinates. If you keep informed on how such changes affect the content of the jobs of your people, you will be better able to plan smooth transitions from past to future conditions.

5. *Plan your communications effort.* Make sure employees receive the information they need to do their work, that associates are provided with the facts they require to cooperate with you, and

that your superior is kept fully informed on progress and developments within your operation. Good communications is based on sound, systematic planning.

6. *Analyze your training activities.* Study your training needs, present and future, so that you can plan a thorough, result-getting training program that will help employees develop the skills and flexibility they should have to move quickly and efficiently from one job assignment to another and thus carry out your plans properly.

7. *Keep an eye on operations.* Operations should be constantly checked so that you can plan new ways to increase efficiency and lower costs.

8. *Move forward on your self-development program.* Self-development must be a thorough, continuing process if it is to attain results. Plan how to reach your objectives by deciding what courses you need to take and what publications or books you should read to learn more about your job today—and tomorrow. Knowledge is the key to good planning for each phase of your responsibilities, and planned self-development is the straight path to knowledge.

THREE

How to Build Good Teamwork through Better Communications

Andrew Jackson fought the Battle of New Orleans after the War of 1812 was over. Neither he nor his opponent, Gen. Sir Edward Pakenham, had gotten the message that a peace had been concluded between the United States and Great Britain. General Pakenham paid with his life for this absence of communications. So did many other soldiers.

Napoleon was on his way to exile on the island of St. Helena after the Battle of Waterloo. His defeat, and it cost him his empire, might have been a victory if he could have sent word to Marshal Marquis Emmanuel de Grouchy. The latter, with troops Napoleon badly needed, was chasing a supposedly retreating Prussian army which had backtracked and already arrived to join in Wellington's victory.

When General Dynamics lost a record $425 million in two years, poor communications, said a critic, contributed to this disaster. There was little communications or cooperation among any of its nine divisions.

One of the first signs of coming catastrophe for a nation, an army, or a company is a breakdown in communications. When this happens, coordinated action is impossible, leaders make independent decisions without regard to the effect of their decisions on others, and ordinary people, lacking firm, positive leadership, become apathetic and give up hope.

The foregoing illustrations are instances of what happens when the administration of an organization begins to disintegrate and communications is no longer possible. However, minor examples of poor communications occur in every company almost every day. Sometimes the results are serious—and expensive! How often have you seen things go wrong—schedule breakdowns, misunderstood orders, departments working at cross purposes—all because somebody withheld information, gave the wrong information, assumed that certain people who were supposed to have been told had been told, or issued instructions that were misunderstood and failed to follow up until it was too late?

Yes, sound communications is a master key to a company's success. A noted management consultant remarked, "The quickest and best way to evaluate the effectiveness of an organization is to check the efficiency of its communications system."

COMMUNICATIONS: THE INDISPENSABLE TOOL

The American Management Association has reported that a supervisor spends at least 90 percent of his working time communicating one way or another. Analyze your job assignment and ask yourself, "What activity that is related to the supervision of my subordinates can I perform without communications?" The answer is very plain. There simply is not any. You communicate when you make job assignments or give instructions. Training depends on communications. The adjustment of grievances and complaints requires talent in communications, as does the conduct of an appraisal review or an employment interview.

The truth of the statement, "If you can't communicate, you can't manage," becomes apparent. Communications is an essential tool in developing an achievement-oriented, highly motivated employee group. It is an indispensable talent in a leader.

Many managers remain indifferent communicators because they never really learn what are the ingredients of good communications. The ability to use words effectively may not be enough. Some highly articulate managers somehow or other fail to win the trust and confidence of their subordinates, who doubt their bosses' job knowledge, judgment, credibility, or firmness of purpose and so do not put trust in the bosses' words.

The capable supervisor knows that his credibility as a communicator is in direct proportion to the trust employees have in his integrity. When workers have learned from experience that any information the boss gives them is factual and accurate, that he never attempts to mislead them or gives them delaying answers that merely postpone the breaking of bad or unpleasant news, the climate in which good communications can operate has been established. Without mutual confidence between the communicator and the listener the best techniques, the most highly developed skills, either written or spoken, are of little value. The barrier of skepticism that has been built by what the manager says as compared with what he does seals off the flow of two-way communications.

Good two-way communications is the foundation of high morale. Although it may be true that under certain conditions obedience, or a semblance of it, may be compelled, cooperation must always be voluntarily given. It cannot be ordered. Furthermore, a supervisor can expect employee cooperation to be given or withheld in direct proportion to the confidence subordinates have in his leadership and to their pride in the group of which they are members.

The skilled communicator works at his job constantly. His instructions are logical and clear; his adjustment of complaints shows that he has a good understanding of the problems. He is always willing to explain to his subordinates the reasons for his decisions. When counseling an employee, he is understanding and makes a positive effort to be helpful. Always approachable, he is ever willing to listen to the ideas, suggestions, and troubles of employees, but he has learned how to do this efficiently and without wasting time.

Communications is hard work, and some managers slack off in their communications responsibility with the excuse, "It takes too much time that I need for other things." A supervisor with this attitude usually has time for everything connected with his job except employees. In a sense, he is still a "doer," not a manager. When you work with machinery or tools, you know what to expect. But people are not machines. They are balky. They want explanations. They do not always accept decisions blindly. They want to be consulted and have their ideas considered. They are resentful when treated as part of the equipment, robots paid to do a job and expected to do what the boss orders with no questions asked.

Self-discipline is extremely important in communications. There are many managers who use language remarkably well to say very little. Clarence Randall, former president of Inland Steel Company, observed, "Too many people turn on the spigot before they look to see if there is any water in the tank." Unfortunately, talking first and thinking later is an all-too-human fault. Good communications must be thought out in advance, just as sound planning must precede effective action. When a supervisor tries to talk before he thinks, or when he plans and acts simultaneously, he is almost certain to cause confusion and misunderstanding which impede operational efficiency.

A leading company executive explained, "A boss can fool associates, and even his superiors, for a time. But not subordinates. Their view of his leadership is from the bottom-side, where it is hard to conceal the flaws and hide the patches. No boss ever really becomes one until employees confirm his title by their support, and that they never give him until he convinces them that his judgment is sound, his decisions are usually right, and it is in their interest to help him push them through to success."

WHAT AN EMPLOYEE EXPECTS

While methods of leadership cannot be standardized and the approach that works for you may be ineffective for somebody else, most good supervisors and executives recognize that communications is essential to successful leadership and are careful not to neglect it. They strive to satisfy the desire of their subordinates to be appreciated as important, contributing members of the group, and they are well aware of the value of acknowledgment and prompt reward for superior performance.

So what does an employee expect of his boss? Glance at the following items and you will see that the ability to communicate is a necessity if a supervisor hopes to satisfy the requirements of his subordinates.

1. An employee expects to receive whatever training is necessary to enable him to meet the performance standards of the company. He looks to his boss to give him that training.

2. An employee wants to know precisely what yardstick the supervisor is using to measure his performance. He expects his superior to tell him.

3. An employee wants to be told how he is doing—whether his work is satisfactory. Only the supervisor can give him this information.

4. An employee expects to go to his supervisor for advice and counsel on job-related problems.

5. An employee expects to take his grievances or complaints to his boss. Adjusting such matters requires a high skill in communications.

6. An employee is disappointed and resentful if his superior fails to recognize him and show appreciation for a good job or for a suggestion that improves overall operations.

7. An employee expects his superior to keep him informed, explain changes in company policies, rules, and practices, and in general keep him up to date on facts that relate to his job or working conditions.

8. An employee desires a positive working environment that allows him to mix freely with other members of his group and be accepted and respected and a producing member of it.

9. An employee may not say so in exactly these words, but he works hard for a boss who is sincerely interested in his progress and with whom he can discuss day-to-day problems that relate to his work.

10. An employee expects his boss to be a leader, to accept responsibility for his decisions, and to protect the legitimate interests of his subordinates.

HOW TO STEP UP PRODUCTIVITY BY BETTER COMMUNICATIONS

Complex and thorny problems offer new challenges to American business which must be met and surmounted if the United States is to remain an affluent nation. Speaking of the supervisor's role in meeting this challenge, the president of one large company observed,

> He [the supervisor] has a tough job ahead. He has to help management make employees understand that security rides on their contribution to organizational competitiveness; that quality and efficiency of product or service are the only means of assuring the continuation of jobs. Getting this message to employees requires leadership, and the responsibility of leadership is the job of management, the job of the supervisor.

James Roche of General Motors echoed these thoughts when he commented,

Our ability to improve our standard of living depends directly on our willingness to work to create the goods and services we enjoy. Productivity is reduced fully as much by poor quality output as by no output at all. Moreover, we are finding that quality of workmanship is falling off at the very time that customers are expecting higher quality.

These are hard, brass-tack facts. To attain the objective of greater efficiency and higher productivity, intelligent, realistic communications is imperative. Communications is the thread that holds the cloth of the organization together; it is the nervous system of achieving management. The following checklist may be useful in upgrading the morale of your subordinates and improving productivity.

1. *Fill your think tank full before you turn the communications spigot.* Poor instructions are the root cause of many failures in communications. If a supervisor gives orders that are too general, too open-ended, inaccurate, or too vague to be carried out properly, he cannot expect to get results. If you study a particular job until you have a firm grip on its details, and then plan how to give instructions carefully, you will have little trouble in explaining your wishes to employees, or they in understanding what you want done.

2. *Tailor what you say to the needs of the individual employee.* If you have a personal relationship with your employees, you understand how each reacts to a given situation. Such knowledge sharpens the edge of communications and is an invaluable asset to you in selection. You know which employees respond to pressure jobs as challenges, which ones need encouragement and reassurance in emergencies. You can communicate in such a way as to build the confidence of the insecure. You make it a practice to explain patiently to the slow learner and to point out problem spots to the impulsive subordinate who is likely to trip over details. Because of your attention to people your orders gain weight by your own assurance, and your confidence is mirrored in the confidence of your group.

3. *Be objective and clear in communications.* The book *Front-line Management* advises supervisors to be objective and clear in establishing their communications goals, and provides this further advice:

> Before you begin to communicate, ask yourself, "What do I want to accomplish?" Are you seeking facts? If so, decide what information you require so you can ask intelligent, precise questions. Do you want to make an assignment? Make certain you have analyzed the job thoroughly so you can explain it properly. Are you faced with a discipline problem? Be satisfied that you have investigated the case and have full information on it before you reprimand or penalize. Are you trying to counsel an employee in order to persuade him to change his ways? Try to get him to talk, and listen to what he says. Don't try to communicate too much too soon. If your goal is sharp, clear and near, you have a better chance of reaching it.*

4. *Follow communication with action.* "Put your money where your mouth is," is the familiar challenge to the person who is big on talk, slow on action. Movement must follow words, or the most convincing language soon becomes wasted effort. The entire purpose of giving orders is to launch employees into planned and co-ordinated movement to achieve a desired objective. Procrastination and delay between the time you begin to talk about an assignment and the time you get the work started may persuade subordinates that you are uncertain and lack confidence in your own decision.

5. *Suit the method to the occasion.* What you say and how you say it determines the reception of communications, but how to choose the right way to communicate particular information to employees at a particular time depends on the demands of the occasion. There are circumstances when the peremptory order is exactly what is needed. There are other situations in which a supervisor must encourage employees and build their confidence if he wants their best response. Your mood may also affect your manner, tone of voice, or attitude and hurt your ability to com-

* J. M. Black and G. B. Ford, *Front-line Management*, McGraw-Hill, New York, 1963, p. 108.

municate. Sometimes the way you feel causes you to withhold the spirit of the message despite the fact that you give it words. It is not what you say but how you say it that shapes results.

6. *Be sure of your facts and of your authority.* Make certain anything you tell employees about the company's practices, policies, or plans is based on solid fact. When you do not have the answer to a question, simply say so. At the time tell the employee you will try to get one. A subordinate does not expect you to be all-knowing, but he does expect honest answers. Also, do not discuss a subject unless you are the right person to do the talking. Unauthorized communications based on guesswork, wishful thinking, or the desire to be important has caused difficulties for many managers and their companies and is an important reason why so often the grapevine flourishes like the green bay tree.

7. *Take an interest in the development of subordinates.* Such an attitude creates a positive employee climate that will help you "sell." If people believe that you want to give them information, instruction, and counsel that is helpful, what you say about other matters carries more authority.

8. *Develop your listening skills.* This is the best way to convince a person that you are interested in him. The act of listening persuades employees that you respect their opinions and will give a fair hearing to their ideas and suggestions. The boss who makes himself available and encourages subordinates to talk learns much that is useful about them and what is going on in his department. As a bonus he also learns how to do his own job better.

9. *Never neglect follow-up.* A good system of controls is essential to every management activity, especially communications. The job is only half done when you send the message. Never take it for granted that a subordinate unfailingly understands your instructions or comprehends perfectly a new policy or a new work procedure simply because you have told him or posted a notice about it. Check to make sure.

10. *Keep subordinates informed on future plans.* Answering

questions and explaining immediate operational plans is important, and you spend a good part of your working day doing just that. However, the "look-ahead" boss does not become so involved with the present that he forgets the future. He knows that employees like to be informed of new plans or developments that may affect their jobs or working conditions. There is nothing like being "in the know." The leader who takes the time to tell employees of long-range plans soon discovers that the rewards are high in terms of increased interest in attaining future goals. Objectives become clearer and employees have a greater sense of participation. Furthermore, resistance to change is lessened to a remarkable degree.

COMMUNICATIONS AND YOUR LEADERSHIP JOB

Psychologists observe that job satisfaction is comprised of three ingredients. They are:

1. *Material requirements.* The paycheck plus its accompanying fringe package satisfies the material man. Money and the various benefit programs such as pensions and insurance underwrite the employee's security and permit him to support his family and himself pleasantly and comfortably.

2. *Social requirements.* There are relatively few "loners" in society. The average person likes to be an accepted and respected member of his own group and takes pride in belonging to an organization that is itself a successful enterprise.

3. *Personal requirements.* Mark Twain once wrote that the law of work provided that the more a person enjoyed doing his job, the more he was likely to be paid for it. It is human for an employee to want to believe that his job is important and to know that his boss appreciates his effort and gives him credit for his accomplishments.

Any subordinate who considers his job drudgery probably seeks self-fulfillment in other kinds of activities, some of which can be quite detrimental to harmonious employee relations. To create a positive employee relations climate a supervisor must provide leadership based on an understanding of the individual needs of people who make up the group.

The objective of a company's personnel program is to furnish compensation, benefits, and working conditions that add up to job satisfaction for the average employee and to establish group activity. But "satisfiers" such as high wages and liberal benefit plans will never justify their cost if supervisory leadership is deficient.

The ability to communicate by word and example is an all-important skill of the successful manager. When management provides the kind of leadership that builds group pride in organization that results in company accomplishment, you may be certain that an efficient communications system is in operation. For good communications fosters a spirit of teamwork among employees, and a boss who has the cooperative support of his subordinates is doing his communications job.

Here is a set of guidelines which may be helpful to you in using communications to secure employee cooperation and support for your leadership.

1. *Be the boss.* Subordinates expect the boss to live up to his responsibilities of leadership. They make three basic demands: a supervisor must (*a*) be technically equipped to do the job; (*b*) treat subordinates fairly; and (*c*) recognize and reward outstanding performance. Employees understand that a supervisor is a representative of management, and they want just that, not a fellow employee. The boss who attempts to win easy popularity by dealing with subordinates at their level and by being "one of the gang" is likely to lose what a boss needs most—respect. If you are the leader, you call the turns and make the tough decisions. It is your responsibility to ask the best from employees and to provide the type of leadership that makes them want to give it.

2. *Be tough-minded, not tough.* It has often been said that em-

ployee attitudes mirror their boss's. The hard-nosed manager who tries to lead by fear may compel obedience, but in doing so he destroys initiative and cooperation. The supervisor whose subordinates "go by the book" and carry out orders literally is storing up trouble for himself. A good leader makes tough decisions and solves hard problems, but he always knows the difference between tough-mindedness and being tough and is fair and consistent in his relationships with employees.

3. *Be proud of your team.* Subordinates underwrite your success. The leader whose subordinates give him the most support gives them the most in leadership. Such a leader always credits his team members for the results he achieves through their efforts. While he may reprimand a subordinate for an error or a shortcoming, he is quick to defend his people from outside criticism. Well aware that a well-trained work force gives him more time to devote to planning and directing overall operations, he is a patient instructor and a good communicator. Employees, realizing they have the confidence of their superior, repay him by cooperation and intelligent initiative.

4. *Encourage participation.* No matter how good you are, you cannot do everything yourself. Employees soon let the boss who thinks he has all the answers know that he has not even asked some of the important questions. The supervisor who trusts his subordinates and encourages them to make suggestions manages in a relaxed climate and employees are not afraid to think for themselves. Communications flow easily. Subordinates do not feel shut out of the decision-making process. A leader who asks for employee participation in certain kinds of problem solving has found the key to cooperation.

5. *Don't dodge hard decision making.* There are times when you want employee participation in decision making, but there are also times when the decision is strictly up to you. In emergencies you cannot ask for a show of hands or worry about employee reaction. Make the necessary decision promptly and confidently and

subordinates will back you to the hilt. They realize you are faced with a crisis, and their trust in your judgment gives them confidence that what you are doing is the right thing to do.

6. *Give employees your trust.* Trust is a two-way street. The man who knows you are relying on him usually responds and does his best to justify your faith.

7. *Identify objectives.* You may have heard the story about the work gang which was told to dig postholes five feet deep behind an industrial plant. No reason was given. Very soon the workers quit and angrily demanded an explanation for what seemed to them useless labor. The reason was simple. The company had lost a construction blueprint and was trying by exploratory digging to trace a network of pipes so that necessary replacements could be made. When the explanation was given, the men returned to work. Employees want to know why they are working and to what end.

8. *Be on the lookout for danger signs.* Be familiar with the pattern of attitudes and job habits of employees. That way you are quick to detect changes in moods or practices. When a subordinate seems out of sorts, hostile, or resentful, talk to him and learn what the trouble is. Preventive maintenance in human relations is secured by intelligent communications and helps assure cooperative attitudes.

9. *Eliminate irritants.* When an employee complains about working conditions and job problems or makes suggestions which he thinks will improve operations, give him an attentive hearing. Then say what you can do about the difficulty or give him an explanation if action is either impossible or not feasible. You may find reasons why the employee has not always been cooperative in the past. This will enable you to change your approach in dealing with him and help him become a more satisfactory subordinate.

10. *Be frank and honest with employees.* Sometimes you have to talk to a worker in plain, no-nonsense language. As boss you cannot escape this responsibility. So never use let-him-down-gently

words when the occasion requires a stern rebuke. Such an approach may so cushion your intent with kindness that the employee misses your meaning and hardly realizes he is being reprimanded.

LISTENING—THE RECEIVING END OF COMMUNICATIONS

Unfortunately, when the average person thinks of communicating he automatically assigns himself a role at the talking or sending end. Certainly there is no lack of human transmitters of communications. But good receivers? They are not so easy to find. The manager who spends all of his time perfecting his sending set is neglecting half of his responsibility. Listening is essential to the success of a communications program, and it is absolutely necessary in two-way communications.

If you send the message and do not know whether or not it is heard, you may be wasting your time. Scientists on this planet have frequently tried to transmit messages into space to discover whether they could make contact with intelligent beings on other worlds. Up to now this effort has been a one-way street. Whether anybody ever received the messages is not known. But this much is known. Nobody has ever replied.

The talented listener can become a perceptive and able boss. Employees talk to him easily, and the information they supply makes his own communications effort more effective.

Developing listening talent takes patience and practice. A high official of the Franklin D. Roosevelt administration had one outstanding attribute that helped him climb the ladder of State Department success: "He could listen intelligently in seven languages." This skill made him invaluable to the President, who wanted to know what was on the minds of such then powerful world leaders as Mussolini, Hitler, and the military junto that ran Japan. All the President had to do was to send this man to talk to a nation's leader, and in a skillful interview this man would encourage that leader to give him the information Roosevelt needed.

Developing listening talent takes patience and practice. Here are some suggestions that experts say will help you:

1. *Learn to concentrate.* The wanderlust mind is an enemy of good listening habits. When the other fellow is talking, do not let your mind take a lazy stroll down memory lane. Concentrate on what he says. Good listening requires mental discipline. Next time your boss makes a report at a departmental meeting, see if you can remember what he said. Take no notes; simply rely on memory. At your first opportunity after the meeting reconstruct his remarks by writing them down on paper. It may be hard at first, but by practice you can develop your powers of concentration and in doing so improve your listening habits.

2. *Ask questions when you lose a train of thought.* No one can maintain peak listening efficiency for very long. Questions will fill in the missing pieces of a communicator's message and protect you and him against later misunderstandings.

3. *Catalog the main points.* Always try to identify the main points. That way you can quickly understand the importance of the speaker's remarks. If you allow your thoughts to be confused by detail or buried in a pile of irrelevant information, the speaker's main message has missed the target.

4. *Hear the speaker out.* A poor listener frequently is so busy preparing his remarks for the next time he is able to seize the floor that he hears nobody except himself. If you constantly cut across conversations to make corrections, or if you constantly take exception to certain points a speaker is attempting to make, you do not give him a chance to clarify his ideas. Constructive communications is impossible, and the conversation degenerates into a series of useless verbal exchanges.

5. *Do not be influenced by your personal opinion of the speaker.* Strive for objectivity. Personal prejudice can destroy your

ability to listen. Even if you do not like a communicator and although you disagree with his ideas, you cannot debate his ideas effectively unless you know precisely what they are. So do not permit bias to lessen your ability to give the other person his chance to say his piece or your ability to hear and understand it.

6. *Be certain you know the meaning of the speaker's words.* If you do not understand a speaker's use of a word, or if his language is not clear to you, ask him to redefine his statement. Words often have several meanings, some of which you may not know. Language can be used to confuse as well as to clarify. People hesitate to challenge the use of profound terms, and "bafflegab" experts have always capitalized on this timidity. So if you hear someone come up with a linguistic lulu like, "The implementation of behavioral indices extraneous to the functional interdependence of variable role perceptions is extrapolated from the motivation interplay," ask what the devil he is talking about. A fed-up listener, hearing this very same pompous collection of words, bravely put his ignorance on the line and snapped, "What does all that malarky mean?" "Not a thing," replied the speaker. "I just wondered if anyone would ask me!"

HOW TO KEEP COMMUNICATIONS PIPELINES UNCLOGGED

Just as fast-moving up-and-down communications is a sign of an efficient organization, poor communications is the flashing red warning signal to a company that there is trouble ahead. A competitive organization simply cannot prosper if its communications is faulty.

The dinosaur went out of business in prehistoric times because its communications system was so sluggish that it could not compete with other creatures in the fight for survival. Authorities say that if you hit the big reptile a heavy blow on the tail, it took twelve seconds for its brain to get the message, and this was too much of a handicap to allow it to compete. So despite its strength the dinosaur was soon deposited on Nature's junk heap.

However, the "dinosaur mentality" still exists (judging from the attitudes and methods of some managers). Although communications pipelines in their organizations are clogged with the rust of indifference, complacency, or a "what they don't know won't hurt them" point of view, such managers do not seem to recognize the many problems that are crowding in on them and soon it will be too late for them to deal with them at all.

Communications is affected by many conditions—by the feeling of the sender and the mood of the receiver. Moreover, words themselves are not perfect carriers of thought. A particular word may mean one thing to one person and something entirely different to another. Attitude, gestures, or tone of voice may convert what is seemingly a straightforward order into a threat, or an employee's acquiescence to instructions into insubordination. The classic illustration of this is Owen Wister's Western hero, "the Virginian," who, on being called a name that reflected on his ancestry by a hard-drinking gunhand, quietly replied, "When you call me that, *smile!*"

The human factors that interfere with communications are as many and varied as human nature itself. Such negative qualities as indifference, jealousy which results in departmental or personal rivalries, complacency, fear which causes uncertainty and lack of confidence, and impulsiveness all bring about breakdowns in communications. Negative attitudes form barriers against which the most persuasive words have little impact. The set of mind of the listener will determine whether or not he goes along with what you say. If he has preconceived opinions or thinks that what you are telling him is self-serving or against his interest, fact and logic will do little to convince him otherwise.

Good attitudes are the best insurance against employee dissension and they help you keep communications pipelines open and ready for traffic. Here is a checklist that may help you clear your communications channels.

1. *Encourage organizational pride.* Most employees want to take pride in their department and their boss, because in doing so they can take pride in themselves. Good communications, supported by sound supervisory leadership and performance, provides the foundation for company pride.

2. *Recognize the job well done.* Honest and swift praise for accomplishment should be automatic if a communications system is to work properly.

3. *Develop the ambitious.* Opportunity for promotion must be available to all employees. But the desire to move up to more challenging assignments is stronger in some subordinates than in others. If a good worker thinks he is blocked off in a dead-end job, he will become an indifferent performer or will simply leave the company. If you show employees that you are sincerely interested in helping them realize their ambitions, that you are glad to work with them to improve their abilities, you give credibility to your communications. But if they believe you do not care and are merely using them to get the day's work done, they will not be too receptive to anything you say.

4. *Guard the reputation of the company.* Credibility of communications is based on two-way trust. Actions speak louder than words. If your practices and leadership methods do not correspond with what you say, great verbal skill and exceptional communications talent may be wasted. Employees generally form their opinions of what a company says (and its decisions and policies) by what their boss says and does. To protect your company's reputation and your own integrity, you must practice what you preach.

5. *Settle complaints quickly.* Unsettled complaints are a sign of communications breakdowns. If you put a grievance on the back burner with the thought that you will attend to it when you have more time, you are taking a serious risk. If a complaint has merit, the employee should be given immediate relief. If it does not, he

is entitled to an explanation. The boss who knows how to handle complaints promptly and properly wins the respect of subordinates and keeps communications flowing in regular channels and his department out of the rumor factory.

6. *Be consistent.* Employees want to know how they stand, and they cannot know this unless they know how you stand. Inconsistent, unbalanced leadership methods are certain to cause anxiety and uncertainty. Such attitudes are barriers to good performance.

7. *Keep communications flowing upward.* You need to know what is on the collective mind of employees. Encourage suggestions—solicit employee ideas and participation, when appropriate, in solving operational difficulties. If you are available and receptive to their opinions, workers will respond by providing you with a full knowledge of day-to-day operating conditions, tip you off on potential problems, and work with you to take preventive action. Mutual understanding creates an organizational atmosphere in which effective communications can almost be taken for granted.

COMMUNICATIONS—ASSIGNMENT IN LEADERSHIP

Communications is involved in every area of management, in every activity. It is the only method you have of working with subordinates. A manager gets his job done by communicating when giving instructions, handling discipline cases, adjusting grievances, or conducting training sessions. Effective communications is the instrument you use to motivate, to build a working team, to win employee cooperation, to sell subordinates on the essentials of giving you full support to achieve departmental goals.

Communications is more than the spoken or written word. It is attitude. Your manner, approachability, and willingness to listen encourage upward communications and permit your enlightenment on employee ideas and problems. Communications is the frame that holds an organization together, and a supervisor increases his ability as a manager as he improves his skill in communications.

When official communications is lacking, members of an organization create their own communications by making their own interpretations of available facts, which are then placed on the company grapevine to circulate as fast-flying rumors. Fear, wishful thinking, and plain dislike of someone or some group are the chief causes of rumors. The only means by which management or a supervisor can minimize the unsettling effect of unfounded gossip that is sure to cause uncertainty and confusion is effective communications. Moreover, it may be too late to counter a rumor if you wait until it has grown so that it is more believable than factual information to employees. Just as Gresham's law applies to money, it also applies to communications: the bad drives out the good. So your communications effort cannot be turned off and then turned on just when you need it. It must be constant and truthful.

Yes, you rely on communications (written or spoken) to do anything that involves people. You cannot direct, organize, or control the activities of subordinates without communications. You cannot get cooperation from supervisors in other departments or keep them informed on matters of mutual concern unless you can communicate with them. Your superior will not know what is going on in your department unless you can tell him.

With so much riding on the ability to communicate well, a manager would be foolish indeed not to take every opportunity to develop this talent. Do not let the seeming ease with which it is done fool you. Simply because you can talk or write a letter or a report you should not conclude that you are a good communicator. To become one you require a variety of accomplishments, including knowledge, patience, understanding, objectivity, and sensitivity to the needs of others. You must also put in hard, steady work.

No, there is no popular "how to do it" book entitled "All You Need to Know about Communications" that you can read in an afternoon that will make your communications responsibility easier or less time-consuming. Nobody can provide you with soft, simplistic solutions to hard communications problems. Nor will you be able to build an efficient communications system overnight that you can start by pulling a switch and then leave the communicating to somebody else. There are no shortcuts. Communications is an assignment in leadership that imposes a continuous responsibility on a manager—that must be worked at every day. If he is successful, the dividends he receives more than reward him for the hours invested. The payoff is an efficient network of communications pipelines through which information moves quickly up, down, and crosswise. The supervisor has done much to assure the efficiency of his own operation and that of his company as a whole.

FOUR

How to Improve Employee Performance through Sound Training Methods

Andy Robustelli was a strong defensive end for the New York Giants who helped spark a steel-hard line that in its day was unequaled in the National Football League. Robustelli became famous for his "search and destroy" mission of the backfields of opposing teams. He had an unerring skill for seeking out an offensive ball carrier and knocking him flat on his back before he could make any threatening gestures toward the New York goal line.

Aside from his superlative ability as a player, Robustelli had other qualities that made him invaluable to the Giants. His leadership on the field was superb, and at practice he was a skillful coach who spent extra hours working with younger players, teaching them the fundamentals of line play and helping them develop his own football know-how, his "can-do" spirit.

"We had a code, and the key to it was the word 'rich,' which we would all be if we made it work," said Robustelli, explaining his coaching role. "R for recognize, I for isolate, C for correct, H for harvest. Players tend to minimize their mistakes. We knew if we could get them to recognize their errors and work to avoid them, we would all benefit. We would win more games and make more money."

Robustelli had a practical, commonsense prescription for success that carried a built-in sales story. He told the New York players, "The well-trained team wins games and shares in the reward." Such an approach to training is the means by which a manager can bring together and develop his people into a cohesive unit capable of working efficiently and cooperatively together to achieve specific objectives. Effective training is the one sure way the manager has to make things happen the way he wants them to happen.

THE TRAINING RESPONSIBILITY

Many a manager has expert job knowledge—the ability to detect performance deficiencies and to know exactly what should be done to correct or eliminate them. But when it comes to passing on this knowledge or skill to subordinates, he fails. Perhaps he lacks patience, perhaps he does not comprehend the learning process. But this quality and ability to train can be acquired. It is well worth obtaining, too. Among the talents that separate the outstanding supervisor or executive from his associates is a systematically cultivated ability to develop competent subordinates. Training is the only method by which this can be done.

Unlike education, training is utilitarian and job-related. In its fullest meaning it includes every phase of employee instruction from the top-level executive seminar to such on-the-job teaching as showing a new machine operator how to operate his equipment. Training is both a beginning and an ongoing part of every sound personnel program.

Unless they are supported by the effort of efficient employees who properly perform delegated tasks, managers cannot produce efficiently. The average company is well aware of the importance of training, and in the personnel department of a sizable firm

Instruc. Materials
Center

there are staff people who are experts in this field. They are responsible for keeping management informed on developments in training—for example, on programs other companies have introduced that might, with modifications, be adapted to this company's needs. They also help line managers prepare programs that will solve the various training problems which constantly come up in every company. In short, their responsibility is to "train the trainers"—to provide operating managers with the techniques and skills they require to perform more efficiently.

But who are the actual trainers? Who is expected to carry out the job of training on the plant floor? That's right! You are! You, the supervisor! The boss! Who is in a better position than you to detect a deficiency in a person's working methods? Who better than you can take immediate steps to correct it? No one is more qualified than a supervisor to apply Andy Robustelli's prescription for improvement: recognize an employee's error, isolate it, help him correct it, and sell him on the importance of self-improvement, the reward for which is usually a bigger share of the harvest of better results that come from more efficient performance.

The late Gerry Lund, former training director of Otis Elevator Company, described training responsibilities of a supervisor as contrasted with those of a personnel department briefly and clearly when he said:

> He [the supervisor] has the primary responsibility of training subordinates. His technical knowledge of the operation of his department and of the various duties of the different jobs within it ideally qualify him for this function. On the other hand, it is the assignment of a training director and his staff to instruct the supervisor in effective training methods, to help him improve his ability to give instruction, to assist him in identifying training needs and in developing programs to meet those needs either on an individual or on a group basis. But the training staff is not concerned with the day-to-day direct coaching and instruction of employees. That's the supervisor's job.*

* From the author's notebook of comments of executives in industry who participated in the author's seminars.

Industrial training is therefore a joint line and staff effort. The staff people plan and organize the general training program of the company. They instruct managers in effective modern coaching and teaching techniques and provide them with necessary training aids and material. The supervisor, thus trained to be a trainer, is expected to impart his special skills and know-how to subordinates to help them acquire the proficiency they must have to perform their assignments well.

To be successful as a trainer or teacher, a supervisor must develop the following qualities:

He must be patient, realizing that learning is a step-by-step process and that instant results cannot be anticipated.

He must be understanding, trying to adjust his approach to the requirements of the individual.

He must be thorough, making certain his instructions cover everything.

He must be articulate, knowing precisely what he wants to say and carefully choosing the right words to say it.

He must be analytical, constantly seeking to discover employee training needs that require satisfaction.

SUPERVISORY GUIDELINES TO FULFILLING GENERAL TRAINING RESPONSIBILITIES

No welcome mat was laid out for the newcomer to industry in the early part of this century. A retired railroad executive observed:

My first job with my company was that of messenger boy, and much of my time I spent in a busy railroad yard. I'll never forget my first day. The Trainmaster gave me a hard look and said, "So you're the new boy, eh? Well, try not to get in front of an engine for a few days. If you live long enough, maybe we'll teach you how to be a railroader."

Learning how to do a job was certainly more of a do-it-yourself endeavor during the years before World War II. A new worker could expect basic job instruction from his supervisor or from veteran employees, but the training process itself was not as highly organized as it now is. Modern companies know they must have efficient employees to stay competitive. Therefore an important criterion for judging a supervisor is his ability to train a productive group of subordinates. To a large degree, a supervisor's reputation depends on his effectiveness in building a successful working team, and this means he must be able to anticipate future training problems and prepare programs to solve them. His job encompasses a threefold responsibility: he is in charge of supplies, he is responsible for machines and equipment, and he directs the activities of people. But people are his major concern. On the use his subordinates make of supplies, on their skill in utilizing machinery and equipment, depends departmental efficiency, which in turn depends on the quality of the training they have received. The following guidelines may be helpful to you in the organization of your training effort.

1. *Find out what the employee knows.* There is no need to teach a person something he already knows. Your responsibility is to make sure he knows what he says he knows and to train him in what he does not know.

2. *Give a general explanation of job duties before you begin to instruct.* It is essential that an employee have a broad understanding of his assignment before he receives how-to-do-it instruction. So start a job training session with a "why and wherefore" summary of the nature and purpose of his work. With this knowledge as background the employee will learn how to do the job more quickly.

3. *Make certain that training objectives are precisely defined.* The employee cannot score unless he can see the goal. If the objectives are vague or dishearteningly distant, he may give up before he begins. Goals must be set for both the group and the individual. In deciding what goals you think a particular individual should meet, you must evaluate his work first in relationship to its

contribution to the achievement of group goals and secondly in relation to that employee's intelligence, experience, motivation, and present skill.

4. *Build a competitive spirit.* "A team has got to come to play football if it expects to win," remarked a well-known football coach. The same goes for an employee. His receptiveness to training depends not only on his aptitude but also on his attitude and motivation. Remarking on this, a General Electric executive observed that while it was a company's responsibility to provide the training programs and the opportunity for an employee to improve his abilities and develop his talents, whether he did so was a matter he would have to decide for himself. The best training program ever devised will have little impact on a disinterested participant. A good selection program will help eliminate many potentially unsatisfactory employees before they become a problem. But when you accept a person, skillful placement, careful training, and your own example will do much to mold his future attitudes. Two certain ways to kill motivation are to put the employee on a job in which he has no interest and to keep him in the dark about how he is doing on a job he likes.

5. *Do not overtrain.* Too much training—particularly preparatory training—takes the edge off an employee's enthusiasm. He soon thinks that he is always getting ready but never allowed to perform. Repetition is an excellent method of instruction, but if you keep a subordinate doing the same thing over and over again until he gets it 100 percent perfect, he may become bored and the training will become ineffective. Training does not take the place of experience, and no matter how rigorous it is initially, it will not make a new employee's work error free.

6. *Do not judge the employee by your own standards.* A supervisor who sets perfectionist standards for himself and judges his subordinates by them will often be disappointed. Impossibly high standards frustrate and discourage subordinates. Your job is to train average people to do superior jobs, and that is not easy. It takes

persistence and patience to accomplish it. Keep in mind that what seems to you a very easy task may appear quite difficult and complex to an inexperienced employee. A good instructor does not expect miracles. He knows that the average person has to learn to walk before he can run, and the practical standards he establishes are within "stretching" reach of his people so each has a sense of accomplishment when he attains them.

7. *Be realistic.* The more closely and practically you can relate an employee's past experience and training to the problems he will find on a new assignment, the more you will speed up the learning process. Training is functional. It is conducted in a job environment, and the final test the trainee takes to prove his training's worth is always his performance on the job.

COMMUNICATIONS AND TRAINING

Communications and the training function are closely related. Without the first, the second could not exist. Because communications essentially determines your ability as a trainer, this checklist may enable you to fulfill your communications responsibility more effectively.

1. *Welcome employee initiative.* The supervisor who keeps subordinates at arm's length and attempts to call all the shots carries an immense burden. He can never afford to be wrong. But the boss who considers it natural to discuss assignments with employees and get their ideas on how best to do the tasks primes the pump of upward communications. In the process he helps develop employee initiative.

2. *Be sure you know what you want to say before you begin to train.* Successful job instruction is based on sound technical knowledge, clearly and logically expressed. Carefully analyze the job or the method you wish to teach. That way you guard against misunderstandings because you know exactly what you want to say and how to say it.

3. *Make sure the employee understands.* You cannot always take it for granted your message has been received simply because you have sent it. If you have any doubts, ask questions or let the employee explain your instructions in his own words. It is better to be safe than sorry.

4. *Be a trainer, not a faultfinder.* The good communicator uses training to build up an employee, not knock him down. It is always easy to point out what a subordinate does wrong. But to tell him what he does wrong and then how to do it right takes patience, understanding, and a communications approach that is adjusted to his particular needs.

5. *Try to see things from the employee's point of view.* The quality of empathy (the ability to see things in a detached way as they appear to another person) sharpens your skill in communications. When an employee fails to progress satisfactorily, do not simply lecture him. Put yourself in his shoes and ask yourself, "Why? Were instructions clear? Was there follow-up?" Perhaps the cause of his failure is traceable, at least partially, to you. A good communicator judges the quality of an employee's performance on the basis of the quality of the training and communications he has received.

6. *Emphasize the positive.* Use the "how to" approach instead of the "how not to." Constant negative criticism places a wall between a boss and his subordinates. An employee will respond best if you do not simply point out his faults but also help him eliminate them.

7. *Explain why.* When an employee knows why you want him to do a job and why you want him to do it a certain way, he is usually able to master it more rapidly. This does not mean your method is always the best or that an employee should be discouraged from trying to find better ways. But intelligent innovation is based on solid technical knowledge. The person who tries to innovate in a field in which he is an amateur may waste time and wind up rediscovering the wheel. So make sure new people under-

stand the fundamentals of their assignments. Then you can give them a freer hand.

HOW TO RECOGNIZE AND SATISFY A TRAINING NEED

The ability to analyze is an important factor in determining a supervisor's skill as a trainer. True, it is a talent essential to every management function. But in training, the supervisor must not only isolate a training deficiency and develop a plan to correct it, he must also help employees recognize and admit their own mistakes and want to do something to eliminate them.

Personal investigation, observation of an employee's working methods, counseling, talks with subordinates, all help uncover training deficiencies. But there are other useful tools available, for example, department records. They answer such questions as, "Is labor turnover too high? Safety record poor? Housekeeping below standard? Scrap excessive?" A "yes" answer to any one of these questions means you have found a training need.

Another tool is the job description. All you have to do to identify training requirements is to review an employee's job description, item by item, and compare its demands with the reality of his actual performance. In the case of a new employee, the job description provides an outline for his entire training program.

Performance appraisal is also useful in the conduct of day-to-day training and is the foundation of the total employee development program. The appraisal interview should be the preliminary step in any well-rounded training program. In the give-and-take discussion of a good appraisal interview, the employee learns how he stands, what parts of his job he does well, and in exactly what areas of his work he could stand improvement. A constructive appraisal interview creates an atmosphere of understanding between supervisor and subordinate and permits them to work together to solve what in reality are mutual problems. For if a subordinate is functioning at substandard level in one or several aspects of his job assignment, it affects the efficiency of the entire group (of concern to you) and undermines his self-confidence (of concern to him).

When you have found a training need and satisfied yourself as to the probable reason for it, you are ready to begin the next step of the training process, deciding what to do about it. It may be that a simple demonstration is all that is necessary to correct an employee's inefficient job practice. It may be that you will have to develop a detailed program, including individual counseling sessions, to bring about desired changes in work habits or attitudes. If such is the case, you must be familiar with effective coaching and teaching methods and understand how to apply them as each situation demands.

There is an assortment of training techniques, but you must study each training situation as it arises and then determine which technique or combination of techniques will best accomplish your objectives. The following list describes training methods that are most generally used in industry.

1. *On-the-job training.*You are already using this basic learning-by-doing method. Probably 90 percent of the training done in industry utilizes the technique of on-the-job training. You rely on it every time you explain the operations of a job to an employee, show him how to do it, ask him to do it while you stand by to coach, give encouragement, correct mistakes, and at last, when you decide he can do it alone, periodically check or follow up to make sure performance is satisfactory. You use on-the-job training to instruct new employees how to do their jobs or to teach veterans how to work with new or different equipment or apply a new or different work method.

2. *The lecture (classroom training).* "Lecture" is simply a formal name for a talk. It is excellent for group training and is frequently used in conjunction with on-the-job training. You can give several subordinates basic facts about an operation before you show them

how to perform it. The lecture (with a question-and-answer period) is often utilized to explain to employee groups such matters as new policies or changes in policies, changes in job practices, new regulations, or revisions of old regulations.

3. *Vestibule training.* This type of instruction is a form of both on-the-job and lecture-classroom training. The employee receives instruction in special facilities away from the scene of actual production. The technique is very effective in training disadvantaged employees because it gives them time to adjust to the demands of regular working conditions and helps them master the fundamentals of their jobs in an environment free from the pressure of production. Vestibule training can also be used effectively to teach a person how to use a new or different type of machine or piece of equipment; for example, you might use it to train a typist how to operate a Varityper. Since instructors in vestibule training usually work at it full time, you will probably not be responsible for giving such training yourself, but some of your employees may benefit from it.

4. *The demonstration.* This is merely a part of on-the-job training. When you show a subordinate how to do a job by doing it yourself, and then ask him to perform the same task while you observe and coach him, you are using demonstration. This is a basic training tool on which you frequently depend when you must show employees proper work methods.

5. *Job rotation.* The name explains the method. In the shop the employee is shifted from job to job, acquiring greater versatility. Of course, the jobs must be somewhat similar. Rotation may be one answer to work monotony. The employee gains flexibility and is not forced to work on the same repetitive task every day. This sometimes increases a worker's interest in his assignment. However, there is this to remember. The more complicated and specialized an employee's work becomes, the less useful job rotation is. It is hardly possible to switch a highly trained specialist away from his specialty and still get full value from his service.

6. *Written or oral instruction.* When you explain a work assignment to an employee and tell him by what time you want it completed, you are also training him. Instructions are generally given orally, but there are occasions when it is necessary to write them. Written orders should be carefully prepared to eliminate any possibility of misunderstanding. The employee must be able to interpret them accurately. You may not be available to answer his questions.

7. *Delegation.* Skillful selection of employees for job assignments is a valuable training tool. By giving a subordinate new or more challenging jobs you provide him with the opportunity to develop his talents while he "learns by doing." Careful follow-up enables you to give the coaching he may need to prevent mistakes. Wise delegation, accompanied by on-the-job training, is perhaps the best way to build a highly trained, competent group of versatile subordinates who have sufficient flexibility to undertake and accomplish whatever tasks you give them. Such a work force frees you from overdependence on a few key people.

There are many specialized training techniques that have not been included in the foregoing list. Generally speaking, however, they are methods used by staff experts in special situations and are not needed by operating managers or supervisors.

EMPLOYEE ORIENTATION

No discussion of training and training methods is complete if special attention is not given to that very important subject—training the new employee. It is on the soundness of this instruction that future training rests, so it should begin at the start of the first day when the employee reports for work. A subordinate's orientation to the organization and his early training have a tremendous influence on both his attitudes and the speed with which he becomes a productive member of the group. Both must be carefully planned and integrated. The training an employee receives for his first assignment and his introduction to the company are complementary parts of a single program. The following guide may be helpful to you in checking the thoroughness of your own program. It is also useful as an instrument of control that permits you to measure the progress of a new employee and to judge your own performance in getting him started properly.

1. *Create an atmosphere of acceptance.* The welcome an employee receives is important. Make certain that it is cordial and that the newcomer understands right away that you need him and are relying on him to perform valuable service as a contributing member of your team. Be sure he knows that he can count on you to give him, or see he gets, the training he will require.

2. *Describe the training program.* If left to himself too much, a new employee is likely to feel uncomfortable and lost in the shuffle. Don't let this happen. Tell him that a carefully devised training program will prepare him for his job and explain the plan so that he may see for himself that he will take part in a program specifically designed to speed him through the learning period. Implement this discussion with action. If you keep him busy at the beginning, you are starting him out properly and building in him a positive attitude toward his job that will stay with him in the future.

3. *Discuss the organization and work of the department.* Explain how the various jobs relate to each other and how the department fits into the operation of the company as a whole. The employee feels more important if you show him the big picture.

4. *Make introductions.* The new employee is a member of your team. Be certain that he is properly introduced to his associates. The best way to help him feel welcome and at home is to walk the rounds with him yourself. Your very presence tells him that you consider him an important addition to your group.

5. *Give him the company tour.* A tour of the company provides the new employee with a broad understanding of the various

functions. He also needs to be shown the location of such places as the cafeteria, smoking area, rest room facilities or locker rooms, time clock (if he checks in by one), parking lot, and the like.

6. *Explain company rules, regulations, and various benefit programs.* Perhaps the new employee has already received literature on such matters as insurance, savings plans, and the retirement program. He may also have been given an employee's handbook furnishing him with facts on company rules, policies, and other related topics. But it is a good idea to review this material with him. He may have questions he would like to ask. Make certain he gets any literature to which he is entitled.

7. *Make use of the "buddy system."* You have too many responsibilities to devote full time to the training of the new employee. A senior subordinate can help. Be sure you are choosing a person who is qualified by job knowledge, ability to instruct, and attitude. Poor delegation of training duties can undermine an otherwise excellent training program.

8. *Follow up.* An efficient control system is important, especially in training. Every program should be evaluated from the standpoint of results. Improved performance is the best measure of the effectiveness of any training program. Follow-up is a "see-for-yourself" method of control and is particularly useful during the early training of a new employee. Check frequently. Special coaching or instruction will help if the trainee runs into difficulties, particularly if it is accompanied by friendly encouragement.

9. *Keep the new employee informed on progress.* Who is not nervous when he starts a new job? That is the time you can offer the new employee the most help and encouragement. So be available. Answer questions and let him know how he is doing. Your confidence in his success builds his confidence.

10. *Make use of the probationary period.* The probationary period is a final screening device set up to permit management to eliminate employees who have slipped through the hiring procedures but simply lack the ability to meet minimum performance

standards. If a probationary employee does not respond properly to training, and it is perfectly clear that he will never achieve a satisfactory level of performance, you have three choices: (a) transfer him to work he can do if it is available; (b) offer him a lower-rated job whose demands he may be able to satisfy; (c) eliminate him from the organization. The decision should be made during his trial period. You are doing him no favor by keeping him on a job that is beyond his ability in the forlorn hope that some day he may make the grade.

JOB INSTRUCTION TRAINING AND THE NEW EMPLOYEE

In training the new employee supervision generally makes use of the basic, time-tested method of on-the-job training, which is simply another way of saying "learning by doing." This technique is usually called "Job Instruction Training." Its principles are so simple (but so effective) that they can be quickly explained and understood. The plan was used during the Second World War to train literally hundreds of thousands of inexperienced people for jobs in industry (it was part of a general plan developed by the government called "Training Within Industry"), and its success was written in America's unparalleled wartime production.

Job Instruction Training is a four-step course which simply formalizes a teaching process that has always been essential to sound instruction.

1. *Prepare.* The supervisor plans the instruction, making certain that he has the proper facilities and equipment. Preparation includes the creation of a climate in which the trainer secures the trainee's interest in being taught.

2. *Present.* Using actual or mock-up equipment, visual aids, or whatever techniques, such as demonstration, lecture, or illustration, he thinks necessary, the supervisor explains to the trainee what he should know about the job. Key points are stressed, and

by repetition the supervisor makes sure the employee understands each step of the operation.

3. *Perform.* The employee does the work himself under the observation of the supervisor. To make certain the trainee has a clear understanding of his job, the trainer usually asks him to explain why and how he performs the various steps of its operation.

4. *Follow up.* The supervisor permits the trainee to work on his own but inspects frequently to be certain that the trainee is progressing at a satisfactory pace. Follow-up permits the trainer to "eye-check" the trainee's performance and offer advice or show by demonstration how to improve his work, thus speeding up the learning process.

THE DANGER OF TYPECASTING

In increasing your skill as a trainer you may find that one of the biggest difficulties you must overcome is considering objectively the potential abilities of subordinates. Unfortunately, there is the human tendency to stereotype people; for example, "John is good at details but too slow and too methodical to be entrusted with other than routine jobs," "Mary is a fast learner, but careless and likely to make mistakes." The average boss usually has pronounced opinions on the skills, abilities, and intelligence of each of his subordinates. Once this judgment is formed, it is sometimes hard for him to change it.

However, any fair-minded manager will admit there have been times when he gave someone whose ability he thought was mediocre a chance at a demanding assignment (possibly because no one else was available) and that employee did so well that he forced his boss to revise his views on his capabilities. At the other extreme, what supervisor has not known an employee he first thought would be a ball of fire but who buckled under the pressure of competition and fizzled out, revealing undetected shortcomings that heavily overbalanced his attributes? Some people after a slow start demonstrate an amazing capacity to grow; others who are fast starters quickly run out of gas and disappear into routine assignments. Such disappointments and success stories are simply inevitable parts of a supervisor's working life, but they illustrate the moral, "Don't be taken in by first impressions. The real test is long-term performance."

It is your job to study the performance of the people in your group and to rate their abilities, present and potential, so that you can determine what kind of training they need and the method best suited for providing it. Your analysis of the progress an employee is making should be continuous; otherwise you tend to typecast people on the basis of your original judgments and perhaps deny certain subordinates the opportunity for advancement that their actual performance merits. Such an evaluation requires an intimate knowledge of each person in your group. The only objective datum on which you can base your determination of a person's skill or ability is his performance on his present job (in the case of a new employee, the progress he is making in learning a new assignment). This knowledge, plus subjective factors like your evaluation of a person's intelligence, resourcefulness, persistence, motivation, and initiative, helps you form decisions about his value to you and the organization in his present work and his capacity to undertake more difficult future assignments. The more shrewdly you are able to judge the human package and detect signs that indicate he has reached a plateau in his progress or is actually dropping back, the greater will be your ability to develop training programs tailor-made to the needs of each individual in your unit.

THE BASIC PRINCIPLES OF TRAINING

To be effective in training, a supervisor should develop good rapport between himself and the trainees. In the first place, a feeling of goodwill should exist. This encourages the trainees to make an all-out effort to benefit from the instruction because they have been persuaded that they can develop the needed job skills and that this is worth doing. In the second place, reasonable performance standards should be established and carefully explained to the trainees and accepted by them as fair and attainable. Third, a sincere interest in the development of trainees should be shown and demonstrated by encouragement and quick recognition and appreciation of progress. Last, the willingness to give patient, individual training or coaching to persons who require it should be an evident supervisory attitude.

A philosopher said of the world conqueror, Alexander the Great, "His power rested on the fact that he had a liking for differences. He did not expect apples to grow on pear trees." Employees are different in talents, skills, and interests, and a particular employee's attitudes, intelligence, and motivation all play a part in determining his response to instruction. Therefore, as a manager you must learn to diagnose a subordinate's training requirements before you can select the training approach most likely to produce the best results in terms of his later performance. However, you can apply these fundamental training principles in developing all training programs.

1. *Coaching is an individual thing.* Talents and aptitudes vary. A brilliant history student may have trouble solving a simple problem in mathematics. Some employees are quick learners, some take longer. Parts of a job that are easily learned by one person may be difficult for another to master. Even in group instruction the experienced supervisor pays tactful attention to particular employees to make certain they are advancing satisfactorily. Well aware that there is no "one best" training method that can be successfully applied in every training situation, he selects techniques that he considers most likely to get desired results according to the needs of the employee, the situation, and the pressure of the occasion.

2. *Training is progressive.* Training is not a "one-shot" proposition. No single program, however well conceived and conducted, effects a permanent solution for a training problem. Training must

be step-by-step and continuous, with "refresher" instruction provided as required. The step-at-a-time building method of training is especially important in the instruction of new employees.

3. *Repetition is the key to learning.* Few employees learn so fast that they need only a single session of instructions. To make sure a trainee is retaining the information you are giving him, you must test his knowledge (asking questions is one way) and then repeat as necessary to fill in the gaps. This is particularly true of an employee's early training. You cannot take anything for granted. Patience is a quality a good instructor must develop. It pays off for you—and for the trainee—in future performance.

4. *Information on progress is a stimulant.* The employee wants to know how he stands, whether he is making satisfactory progress. You can encourage him and stimulate the learning process by giving him this information. Your genuine interest in a subordinate's development is an almost certain method of building his confidence and instilling in him the will to do even better.

There is nothing difficult or even new about these basic principles of learning, but it takes experience and judgment to apply them properly. Too often pressure of other duties, or perhaps merely the desire to get training over with quickly, causes a supervisor to run into difficulties that proper instruction would have prevented. In such situations the supervisor may have a thorough understanding of the principles of how people learn, but he simply does not want to take the time and make the effort to observe them consistently. The consequences are inevitable. Later he will discover that the poor performance of half-trained subordinates will force him to spend more time and make an even greater effort to correct mistakes or faulty job practices that could have been avoided if sound training had been provided initially. Employee competency does not come quickly. Fundamentals must be taught and learned, and that can only be accomplished through systematic and thorough training.

If you understand and utilize the principles of learning that have been described, and if you know how to apply them to specific situations, you soon acquire great proficiency in selecting proper training methods to meet the various needs of an employee. As this skill develops, you will also expand your range of various kinds of training techniques.

GUIDELINES TO SOUND TRAINING

Training is a never-ending responsibility of management, and to fulfill it properly a supervisor must have ability in carrying out all four of his primary management duties: planning, organizing, testing, and controlling. The following checklist can be used as a guide to make sure you are providing subordinates with the training they require.

1. *Plan training programs carefully.* The value of a training program depends not only on subject matter but also on organization. Faulty planning and inadequate attention to detail have caused many training programs to fail to get results. Before you begin to train anybody in anything, you must decide exactly what you want to do and how to do it.

2. *Instruct clearly.* Precise, intelligent instructions (with frequent question-and-answer checks) are a safeguard against misunderstanding that leads to mistakes and poor job practices. Good instruction quickens the learning process.

3. *Criticize positively.* Try not to humiliate a trainee by letting him see you are unhappy about his rate of progress. Be tactful and help the employee save face. By allowing a sharp tongue to put a cutting edge on your criticism you impede his ability to learn. The employee loses confidence in himself. By showing a sincere interest in his development and patiently correcting his mistakes, you win his appreciation and he will increase his effort.

4. *Explain the job and stress its importance.* An employee can get satisfaction from his work only if he understands that his con-

tribution is important to the overall effort. Every employee should know how his job relates to other jobs, and that you recognize and appreciate the value of his work.

5. *Establish deadlines.* Stress that work should begin and be completed within a definite time frame. Realistic schedules and reasonable deadlines must be established. Such schedules tell an employee your order of priorities, and this knowledge is important in his training.

6. *Make corrections as needed.* If an employee is failing to meet standard, your first job is to find out why. Next you must do something constructive to remedy the situation. Individual training or special coaching may be needed. It could be that a subordinate recently assigned to a new job lacks confidence and needs encouragement. Perhaps the cause of his failure is poor attitude. Or possibly you put him on an assignment that is beyond his skill or experience. Good follow-up reveals problems of this kind before much damage has been done and provides you the opportunity to take corrective action.

7. *Be thorough in inspection.* Inspection gives you firsthand knowledge of what is happening to your department, for example, whether maintenance is up to par, whether safety rules are being followed, and whether housekeeping is meeting standard. Inspection tours also help discover training needs.

8. *Be conscious of the high cost of insufficient training.* No competitive organization can stand the expense of poorly trained, indifferent employees. Their inefficient job practices, lack of motivation, and "don't care" attitudes destroy quality, replacing it with waste, inferior products or service, and higher costs. Training benefits both you and your subordinates. By developing their talents and skills, employees move up to better opportunity. Your reputation rests on the level of the competence of your subordinates, and you benefit by doing all you can to move that level upward.

SPECIAL TRAINING FOR THE DISADVANTAGED

Veteran supervisors who began their careers in the 1950s or before sometimes have difficulty in managing relatively new entrants into the work force who are popularly described as "disadvantaged." Their supervisory attitudes and practices became fixed in a more stable era, and they look yearningly back to a time when the average grievance concerned wages, hours, or working conditions and when the subtle issue of discrimination because of race, creed, sex, or national origin occurred infrequently. Emotionally they still expect all employees to understand and accept regular working hours, to be able to meet normal job requirements without extra and specialized training, and to share a code of values regarding normal behavior. These supervisors and executives have to adjust to change in order to continue successfully as managers.

The work force is changing dramatically, and today a company offers employment to applicants it would not have hired formerly except for unskilled jobs. In fact, industry does more than just hire such people. It actively recruits them. Many employees of this type are minimally educated and unaccustomed to the discipline of regular work, and their standards of values may be entirely different from those of middle-class society. For example, they might not automatically seek the assistance of an elected union officer (shop steward) in handling their complaints but turn to their own unofficial leaders because they may think that traditional union leadership is part of the so-called "Establishment," and they may resist the authority of the Establishment wherever they encounter it. Frequently they believe they are victims of discrimination when they are simply being asked to obey the same rules and regulations that other employees take for granted.

James L. Blue, writing in *Handbook for Supervisors of the Disadvantaged*, comments:

Many of their [the disadvantaged] job dissatisfactions are simply imagined. The job, because it represents something new and unfamiliar, may be blamed for difficulties unrelated. In any case the grievances are real in the eyes of the individual involved and should be handled as such. A supervisor may often settle a grievance of this kind by allowing the employee to solve his own problem by getting it off his chest. In all cases, whether in the solution of grievances or in other situations in which the employee expresses personal feelings, discussions must be treated confidentially.*

The key to winning the support of such employees and minimizing disciplinary difficulties is to gain their trust. Special skill must be developed which enables a supervisor to reduce clashes of interest between persons and groups. Finally, a basis of common interest must be established which makes the employees feel they are working with the boss and not for him. Companies that have well-rounded programs designed to convert hitherto undereducated, inexperienced people into productive members of their work forces report that when the training takes effect, their record of attendance, their productivity, and their discipline records are about average (for the jobs they are doing), but that early orientation and training is the all-important factor in their eventual success.

The most effective of these programs are based on certain principles which largely have to do with the attitudes of supervisors and the methods they use. A checklist of dos and don'ts may be based on these principles and may help you in your relationship with this type of employee.

1. *Learn that patience is essential.* The disadvantaged employee frequently suffers in the job market because he is environmentally and educationally unprepared and unequipped to meet the de-

* James L. Blue, *Handbook for Supervisors of the Disadvantaged*, State of Washington, Coordinating Council for Occupational Education, Division of Distributive Education, Olympia, p. 22.

mands of disciplined, regularized employment. His vocabulary, standards of behavior, and experience do not fit him to enter an organized work group without preparatory training. A high communications barrier is another obstacle and may make it almost impossible for him to understand simple oral instruction, and written instructions are out of the question because he probably has minimal reading skill and is not able to do simple arithmetic. The life he has led may have given him a chip-on-the-shoulder attitude, which is evidenced by a surly, generally hostile manner toward his new associates and supervisor, all of whom he is inclined to regard as part of a society which is responsible for his deficiencies. He may have a jail record, and the jobs he has held (if any) may have been transitory and menial. In many employees of this kind there is an innate distrust of authority, and supervision represents authority. To assist an employee of this type to become a productive contributor to your work group, you must win his confidence in you and build his self-confidence. Patience is necessary in communications, in training, and in teaching him to accept and live by a new standard of values and with new habits of living.

2. *Locate and develop special skills or talents.* Good placement is the key to the successful absorption of the disadvantaged into a work force. Many of them have potential aptitudes and talents which if properly developed can be useful. But sometimes it takes a perceptive eye to identify them and Job-like patience to bring them out. The disadvantaged person is accustomed to failure, and if assigned to a job he has difficulty doing he is likely to become discouraged quickly and quit or cause disciplinary trouble. He simply lacks the persistence to continue an effort he thinks has no chance of success. He requires assistance and frequent encouragement. If he is over his head, he may not trust you sufficiently to discuss the matter, or he may lack the words to describe his troubles. Unlike the traditional employee, he may not actually understand that there is any possibility of asking for a transfer to another job if he dislikes his present one. Somehow you must

find a way to open up the communications channels and reach him. Otherwise you cannot hope to make your training pay off.

3. *Make him feel he is a member of the team.* A sense of "belonging" to the group is a requirement for job satisfaction and it must be developed in the disadvantaged worker. If he thinks he is an outside, you can expect sullenness and perhaps disciplinary trouble from him. He has much to overcome. The environment is new and strange. He is being asked to conform to a pattern of disciplined work, and this too may be a singular and first-time experience for him. He has never trained or disciplined his mind, so he may not quickly adapt to a formal, regularized training program. These very real obstacles must be surmounted; otherwise, he may remain hostile to formalized instruction because he feels incapable of mastering it. The handicaps of the disadvantaged create their rebellious attitude. "They make trouble because they are in trouble trying to do work they can't perform efficiently and don't like to admit failure," said one expert. However, many will confess their lack; these have overcome their deficiencies and are now doing excellent jobs. James L. Blue, who has written much on the problems of the disadvantaged, remarked, "They are not dreamers but cynical of theory and idealism. Their way of life has taught them to be practical and realistic. The supervisor who capitalizes on these traits will find that it has great import in training."*

4. *Avoid the moralistic approach.* The disadvantaged are suspicious of the "do-gooder," and they have every reason to be. They have usually had plenty of experience with social planners, social workers, and various other kinds of people who impractically and often (in the mind of the disadvantaged) hypocritically have tried to reform their lives. They have developed a hard shell to protect themselves against moralistic lectures. So if you want them to accept your standards and values, your first task is to try to

* Blue, loc. cit.

understand their problems, their needs, and their ambitions. You must do your best to see things through their eyes so that you can see them clearly as people. By establishing a basis of mutual trust, you may be able to persuade most of them that they will benefit by accepting and profiting from the advantages they are being offered.

5. *Do not expect the disadvantaged to think as you do.* The chronically unemployed person whose payroll department has normally been a relief check frequently lacks a sense of responsibility (as you understand it), and certainly by traditional measures he is undisciplined. He may have no idea of finances and go through his paychecks like a spendthrift, eventually being harassed by creditors. His idea of punctuality may be "so long as you get there sometime," and his attendance may be on a random basis. Considering what his background may have been, you can see why it is necessary for training to include more than just instruction on how to do an assigned task. He must also be taught how to adapt himself to a new way of living, how to work within a disciplined organization, and why it is important to observe various rules governing work practices and behavior on the job. This type of instruction must be given tactfully and with judgment. Such employees resent reprimands and pay little attention to moral preachments.

6. *Supervise with diplomatic thoroughness.* The best method of instructing is on-the-job training. The disadvantaged employee learns by doing, not by reading or by lecture. Encouragement and praise should be given as progress is evident, but your interest must be genuine. Such people are quick to detect an insincere or false note, and they bitterly resent it as patronizing. The more quickly you get to know all employees in your department, both as people and as members of your team, and to work with them on a sound human basis, the better chance you have of maintaining a climate of positive discipline. This statement should be heavily underscored if you are dealing with the disadvantaged.

FIVE

How to Get Results
through Improved Delegation

Delegation is the one act that separates the manager from the "doer." It is the only method by which one person can direct and coordinate the work of many persons. It is the only means by which a manager can broaden his area of action and improve his supervisory capabilities. To develop proficiency in delegation is simply common sense.

To delegate well a supervisor must know how to plan and co-ordinate a variety of activities and how to follow up on their progress. He must decide what responsibilities to retain, which ones will be assigned to subordinates, and which subordinates will be selected for particular tasks. Delegation, therefore, brings into play all of the management functions—planning, organizing, co-ordinating, following up, and decision making.

On the surface, delegation may seem to be the simplest of management techniques, but in reality it is a complex responsibility always accompanied by an element of risk. When you give a person a job to do, you simultaneously give him the authority to make decisions in your name—decisions for which you remain accountable.

WHY SOME MANAGERS ARE POOR AT DELEGATION

Since delegation is so important to supervisory or executive efficiency, why do some managers still try to hang on to all of the details of the operation of their departments? Why do they wish to carry the heavy loads they voluntarily and probably inefficiently shoulder? Attitude, emotional immaturity, lack of confidence in others, vanity, and overconfidence are among the reasons. Here are some of the things managers tell themselves when they fail to delegate.

1. *Who can do the job better than I can?* This point of view marks the expert individual performer who has not learned to think like a manager. He probably can do any particular assignment better than any of his subordinates, hence his reluctance to delegate. But his company is paying him to perform his own job, not a subordinate's. This he cannot do efficiently until he trains subordinates to do theirs.

2. *The job is too important to risk mistakes.* A manager may give employees a vote of "no confidence" without even realizing it. He is afraid that he will be blamed for their mistakes and is worried and uncomfortable in delegating authority. Such a manager may not consciously realize he is withholding responsibility from subordinates and may even think that "most of the time" he delegates well. But a review of his supervisory practices reveals that he tries to keep all major responsibilities in his own hands, that he constantly gives close follow-up to the work of employees, and that (especially in the case of supervisors) he may even create "emergencies" where none exist so that he can take over a

particularly difficult job that would normally be done by an employee.

3. *I feel safe only when I can see what is going on.* This kind of manager lacks an efficient system of controls. Therefore he is naturally concerned about delegation. He relies on visual inspection and standby supervision to keep operations flowing. Since he cannot be everywhere at once, if he has several important jobs that should be performed simultaneously there are likely to be delays caused by his insistence on personal checkups and approval of all activities.

4. *Let's not worry about tomorrow!* Some managers are constitutionally unable to plan ahead. At starting time each morning it is not unusual for their employees to stand around waiting for orders. Such a manager does not plan for the future; he waits until it comes, and then plans or, rather, improvises on the spot. Since he has no real sense of where he wants to go, employees feel their work is purposeless and without guiding direction. This kind of boss may sincerely want to delegate. But because he does not know precisely what is to be done, he cannot determine specifically who will do what. The only work he can assign with any confidence is the routine, mechanical jobs that are part and parcel of every operation.

The supervisor who cannot master the art of delegation often creates additional problems for himself, problems that injure organizational efficiency. His reluctance to delegate probably builds corresponding attitudes in employees: they do not like to accept delegated tasks. Why? If a boss sets himself up as a be-all, know-all authority on every question, why should an employee bother thinking his way to answer the question of how to do a difficult job? It is much easier to reverse the process of delegation and ask the boss to solve his problem. And if an employee has never been given difficult jobs unless the boss is close by to give advice, aid, and encouragement, he may lack confidence to try anything on his own. Also, if a boss is a perfectionist who is severely critical of mistakes, it stands to reason that an employee will shy away from assignments that may expose him to such criticism. Finally, if a boss so lacks confidence in himself that he is unable to give credit to subordinates for outstanding performance and prefers to have all recognition and praise accrue to him, he provides little incentive for employees to undertake hard and complex assignments.

QUALITIES AND SKILLS NEEDED IN DELEGATION

The advantages of effective delegation are so apparent that the inability or lack of desire of many managers to use it properly is almost paradoxical. You are only one individual. No matter how great your ability, your knowledge, and your skill, no matter how much your energy, there are human limitations on what you alone can accomplish. But when you delegate to well-trained employees, you become, in effect, many people and thereby enlarge the scope of your achievement. Your subordinates are your deputies and as such extensions of your will are able to carry out a multiplicity of tasks efficiently and simultaneously.

Of course, you cannot delegate in the manner of the Roman centurion of biblical fame who said that when he told one man to come, "he cometh," and when he said to another to go, "he goeth," unless you expand the order to include "where to come" and "where to go and how to get there." Here are qualities and skills needed to delegate well. You must:

1. *Know the difference between "mine" and "thine."* Acquire a talent for almost "instant recognition" of those parts of an assignment you should keep for yourself and those which you should give to employees. Certain major responsibilities may be altogether yours and so cannot be shared. For example, if serious trouble with a shop steward comes up and he wants to see you, you would be foolish to tell an assistant to handle things while you make an

inspection tour to check on housekeeping. However, that assistant may be perfectly capable of freeing you from the tedious task of reviewing daily production reports and entering them on the record.

2. *Bring judgment to the task.* A thorough knowledge of the skills, talents, experience, and initiative of subordinates is essential to sound delegation. The best way to guard against mistakes is to make certain that employees performing important assignments are qualified to do so.

3. *Assure good controls.* The superhighway to disaster is to delegate and forget. It is foolish to assume that work is being done satisfactorily simply because you told someone to do it. An effective system of controls keeps you informed on progress and tells you whether or not projects are moving forward satisfactorily. Reports (oral or written) and visual inspection are a protection against mistakes. A good control system sounds a warning bell if things are going wrong and sounds it in time for you to make corrections.

4. *Establish limits of authority.* When you delegate a job, you must also delegate the responsibility for doing it properly and the authority to get it done. The employee should understand the comparative importance you place on the assignment, the span of time in which he has to complete it, and the degree to which he is authorized to act in your name. Such precautions prevent a subordinate's abuse of authority or his attempt to expand his authority to a degree you never intended. This last can easily happen if authority is only vaguely defined.

5. *Tell the employee how much follow-up he can expect.* You may delegate a job to an experienced employee and leave him almost entirely on his own to do it, merely asking that he report when it is done. But if you are using delegation as a training device or giving a subordinate an unfamiliar task, let him know that you intend to keep a close check on progress, not because you lack confidence in his ability but to be available if he needs help.

6. *Make delegation an opportunity for two-way communications.* Discuss assignments with employees and get their ideas and suggestions. Before you establish deadlines, set job standards, or tell the subordinate how much authority he will be given to carry out a project, get his opinion on such matters as: How long will the job take? What problems does he foresee in doing it? How much authority does he need to get the job done? Participation in a process usually stimulates an employee's interest. So if you take his views into consideration before making all final decisions, you give him a greater sense of responsibility for doing the work right.

DELEGATION—AN EFFECTIVE METHOD OF TRAINING

There is no better technique of employee training than effective delegation. Many people believe that the only way one can ever learn to manage is by managing, and successful executives frequently attribute their success to a boss they met somewhere in their careers who demanded the very best from them but who gave them important assignments and the responsibility and authority to carry them out. Such bosses know that this is the only true test of training. Certainly there will be mistakes, but good controls will generally prevent too much harm from being done.

On the other hand, so long as a supervisor insists on making every decision himself and following up closely to guard against the possibility of errors, his subordinates have no feeling of personal responsibility for results. If an unusual situation comes up and the boss is not around, they simply attend to routine tasks and wait until he does come to give further instructions. Who wants to risk sticking his neck out? Besides, employees who will put up with such a superior for any length of time have become so accustomed to accepting his decisions blindly they would never take the risk of doing anything on their own initiative.

The freedom you have to delegate depends to some extent on your level in management, as does the importance of the jobs you give to subordinates. But a study of the methods of the majority of highly successful executives reveals that they rely heavily on delegation to attain their objectives and use it extremely well.

Robert Magowan, who is credited with reversing the downward trend of the fortunes of Safeway Stores, remarked of his methods, "For the first time my managers were made responsible for running their own shows. My methods were brutal. Managers were told, 'Here is your chance to produce. If you can't, we'll find somebody who can.' "

Charles Percy also found delegation to be the key to his success when, before he had reached the age of thirty, he became President of Bell and Howell Company. He won the support and cooperation of many older and experienced executives by (said Percy) "giving them responsibility for the first time." He added, "Responsibility brings out the best in people."

Reasons why delegation is so important to the training and growth of employees and for building up their feeling of organizational pride and a belief that their work is essential to group success include:

1. *Delegation is on-the-job training.* You do not know how well a subordinate has learned to do a job until you "cut him loose and let him do it." So long as you stand by to give advice and correct mistakes, his job success depends on you, not on himself. His real development begins when he is asked to assume responsibility for his own assignments. At this point his triumphs and failures begin to form the personal job experience on which he can draw to solve future problems.

2. *Delegation enlarges an employee's skill and increases his versatility.* An employee's assignment to new or different tasks, or a difficult and more demanding job, expands his job knowledge, adds to his flexibility, and raises his self-confidence and his usefulness to the organization.

3. *Delegation can be used to encourage participation.* When delegating, a boss has the opportunity to talk over an assignment with his subordinate and get his ideas on how the work should be done. The employee can express his views on problems he thinks he is likely to encounter, make suggestions on methods, and thus share to some extent in the decision-making process. Participation stimulates interest and a sense of "belonging." Since the boss has the final word, his authority is not weakened. He may accept an idea that has merit, modify suggestions when he thinks necessary, or reject a proposal altogether if he considers it inappropriate.

4. *Delegation spurs initiative.* It makes the employee think. The boss who gives orders in an autocratic manner, who spells out or even shows a subordinate how he wants them accomplished, may be "delegating"—but in a very limited way. He is also enclosing subordinates in a straitjacket of instructions that must be obeyed to the letter. The latter will overdepend on the boss and take little personal responsibility for the operations of their department. Because they have been given no general guidelines which would allow them to act on their own, they simply wait for the boss's directions. But when they have the authority to make certain decisions on their own, their attitude is entirely different. The boss is still the director and coordinator. But within that organizational framework, each person is responsible for the accomplishment of his assignments.

5. *Delegation adds to job satisfaction.* "Variety is the spice of life" is a saying that certainly applies to a person's work. The monotony of performing the same repetitious task day in and day out bores many employees to distraction. This may be reflected in frequent absences and high labor turnover. Most employees enjoy getting out of the rut of the too familiar and respond enthusiastically to new and different assignments.

6. *Delegation identifies training needs.* The ability an employee displays in performing an assignment may be proof that he is well

trained, reliable, and efficient. On the other hand, his errors, his lack of speed, and his uncertainty may indicate training deficiencies which individual coaching or special instruction can eliminate.

7. *Delegation can be used as a reward for work well done.* If an employee performs his work well, he may be ready to take on more difficult and more important assignments. Delegation is the method a wise supervisor uses to provide subordinates a chance to demonstrate their fitness for promotion, and promotion is the delegation of greater responsibility and authority.

METHODS OF DELEGATION

The relationship between the boss and his subordinates creates the climate of delegation in a department. An authoritarian leader may have difficulty in developing successors to run the operation when he departs from it. A capable delegator usually has his replacement ready to succeed him, and there is little loss of organizational momentum in leadership exchanges. By the use of wise delegation responsibility is pushed downward. Employees are encouraged to take part in making decisions that affect them and their jobs. They have a better understanding of their responsibility to the company, to associates, and to themselves. Work becomes more meaningful, for their stake in the company's future is clearer.

There are as many types of delegators as there are bosses, for every manager has his own methods, or combination of methods, of making assignments. But the following profiles of the characteristics of the prototypes of various categories of delegators quickly reveal the strengths and weaknesses of their method.

The Iron Hand   A manager of this type could almost be called a nondelegator. He may be outstandingly capable, just as he thinks he is, but the authority of his subordinates is limited to decision making on routine assignments. Everything else he must approve personally. It is rare that an individual is so talented that he can assume such a heavy burden of responsibility and carry it through to success. But many try. Unfortunately, the so-called Iron Hand often turns out to be a petty tyrant, arbitrary and opinionated, who insists on retaining all authority personally because of his lack of confidence. He attempts to cover his weaknesses by checking everything himself to convey the impression that he is indispensable. He fears competence in a subordinate and considers it a threat to his position. It is no wonder he is afraid of delegation.

The Freewheeler. This type is convinced that the way to develop subordinates is to give them assignments with full responsibility and authority to complete them on their own. If they encounter problems, it is up to them to find solutions. Such a manager delegates broadly, and sometimes too loosely, identifying only the general objectives of a project. Guidelines are frequently vague and two-way communications is not usually encouraged. This type of leader may have tremendous confidence in the abilities of his subordinates and great trust in their judgment and initiative. If this confidence and trust are not misplaced, he can accomplish wonders. But if he misjudges subordinates, the consequences can be unfortunate, for the Freewheeler is not likely to establish an effective control system. If a subordinate makes mistakes, he probably does not find out in time to prevent difficulties.

The Prober. Such a manager considers the question an important tool in delegation and in employee development. A high executive of Continental Can once said, "When you delegate make constant use of the question, 'What do you recommend?'" The question, he said, "puts the burden of solving a problem back on the employee and forces him to try to find an answer." If you ask the right questions, you compel the subordinate to concentrate on his problem and to cover the areas that you wish covered. Therefore the recommendation he finally makes will probably be the one you expected and with which you can agree. But your questions have made the subordinate do his job himself instead of dumping it on your desk.

THE CONSENT OF THE
EMPLOYEES IS NEEDED

The degree to which you delegate reflects your own personality, your belief in your own managerial competence, your confidence in yourself and in your subordinates, and finally, your understanding of your function as a manager. Some managers who make expert use of delegation seem to know instinctively how to get the best out of employees—how to make them respond to challenges and responsibility. They realize that before you can assure the success of delegated work, it must have the consent of its receiver; in other words, the employee must consent to accept the work you are giving him. To win this consent his rights must be respected.

Perrin Stryker, who has written much on management, has described what he calls this "upward" type of authority, and says that it must be recognized by the modern manager. "Upward authority" may be defined as an employee's right to obey, half-obey, or disobey his superior's instructions. If a subordinate freely offers cooperation and does his best to carry out orders properly, he is demonstrating his willingness to grant his boss authority to give him orders. If he only half does the job, if he claims that "things went wrong because instructions were incorrect," or if he in any way frustrates his superior's designs, it may be that he is rejecting an assignment he does not want to do or thinks that he should not be asked to do. If he is clever in his methods, it may be extremely difficult for a superior to do anything about it. He may do his work just well enough to protect himself from being terminated, but that is about all. Eventually he will drive his point home. His long-suffering boss simply gets tired, gives up on him, puts him on routine tasks that do not matter very much, and leaves him there—a drag on the payroll. Of course, if an employee really gets out of line and is truculently uncooperative, he will probably be dismissed. But his boss is admitting his inability to exercise managerial authority and invoking the authority of private property to remove the offender from the premises. "The consent of the governed" is the complementary authority that ultimately controls the success of delegation.

CHECK YOUR EFFECTIVENESS IN DELEGATION

Are you a capable delegator? You can analyze the effectiveness of your techniques by reviewing your relationship with subordinates and your habits in dealing with them. Frank answers to the following questions will help you make this analysis.

1. When a working day begins, do you have ready a program of action that permits you to give assignments to employees quickly and accurately?

2. Do the details of your job occupy so much of your time that you do not have enough left in which to plan properly?

3. Do you frequently have to relieve an employee of an assignment and give it to someone else because a difficult job has come up and he is best qualified to do it?

4. When delegating, do you study the skills, talents, experience, and job knowledge of employees and do your best to match their attributes to the demands of the various tasks?

5. If an employee does a particular type of assignment well, do you keep him on it instead of trying him on anything else?

6. Are you frequently so tied down by the details of your job that you lack the time you need to supervise employees and follow up on their activities?

7. When emergencies occur in your operation, do you and your employees handle them with sureness and confidence?

8. In following up on the efficiency with which an employee

accomplished an assignment, do you take note of training needs that may be revealed by his mistakes or work practices?

9. When employees report to work, do they wait for your instructions or begin automatically on their assignments?

10. Is your employee group smoothly efficient and cooperative?

11. Do you often fail to meet deadlines because employees take too long to finish their tasks?

12. Do you fall back too many times on the excuse to explain failures, "Things just didn't go the way I had planned"?

13. Do trivial jobs seem to take forever?

14. Do employees keep their ideas and suggestions on job methods and working conditions to themselves?

15. Do subordinates "go by the book" and carry out your instructions with mechanical deliberation and a revealing lack of enthusiasm?

The right answers are obvious. The questions are intended merely as a checklist. Even the best delegator will admit that there are occasions when he has to answer any one of the foregoing questions negatively. But then nobody is at peak ability all of the time. However, if a manager generally follows good delegation procedures, he will be all right. The department's work will be properly allocated, priorities will be in order, and highly efficient employees will not complain that they are always loaded down with work while others appear to get by while doing relatively little.

In a working climate created by intelligent delegation, morale is usually high, employees are self-reliant and responsive, and the boss has time to attend to his essential duties—planning, directing, coordinating, and following up on the activities of his subordinates. The following suggestions may be helpful in making sure that you are using good methods of delegation and improving your skill in this essential managerial responsibility.

■ When you delegate a new or different assignment, make certain that you accompany your instructions with any information the employee needs regarding company or departmental policy or procedure relating to the work.

■ Be sure to tell a subordinate precisely what the limits of his responsibility and authority are in carrying out instructions. Check to make certain that his understanding of these limits is the same as yours.

■ Delegate fairly and do not overload key subordinates with a multiplicity of assignments because you know they will perform them well while you keep others with the same potential ability in mechanical or routine jobs.

■ Do not allow an employee to reverse the delegation process and force you to do his work for him. Do your best to make him reach his own decisions, even if at first you have to guide him to those decisions with questions. Do not accept unfinished work from a subordinate and complete it yourself. It is your job to see that he does his job.

■ Give-and-take discussion to develop the initiative of employees and encourage their participation in certain parts of the decision-making process is helpful in the delegation process.

■ Use delegation to detect training requirements and then apply the corrective training.

■ Do not keep an employee on a particular type of assignment simply because he does it well and it is easy that way. His excellence on the job he is doing entitles him to your consideration for more responsible work or promotion.

■ Do not publicly countermand a subordinate's instructions (unless there is a grave emergency) and destroy his self-respect. If it is necessary to change his orders, tell him privately and ask him to straighten the matter out.

■ Support subordinates and protect them from outside criticism. If an employee is not doing an assignment properly, correct him. But back him up if he has difficulties with other managers. However, do not permit the subordinate of another manager to come to you directly to get a decision reversed. Lines of authority should be respected.

■ When an employee needs help, try to assist him, not by giving answers, but by showing him how to find the answers himself.

■ Keep communications open. They are your day-to-day controls over delegated authority.

■ So far as your superiors are concerned, never try to escape responsibility for a delegated assignment by blaming a mistake on the subordinate who actually did it. After all, you selected him.

■ Use delegation as a training tool. By giving an employee different or more difficult assignments, you increase his versatility, stimulate his job interest, add to his experience, and help him improve himself.

■ Follow up. Follow-up is part of your control system, and good controls enable you to do something about mistakes in the making.

SIX

How to Supervise a Positive Discipline Program

"Liberty," a wise Frenchman observed, "is a luxury of the self-disciplined."

It is certainly true that many people who refuse to discipline themselves eventually have discipline imposed on them. The American system of competitive enterprise has endured hitherto because of the general self-discipline of its citizens and the Puritan-pioneer belief in the principle of work with its reward to the individual for creativity and for ideas that advance his own and the country's economic progress.

A CHANGE IN ATTITUDES AND ITS IMPACT ON INDUSTRY

The 1960s, however, witnessed a startling change in many traditional American attitudes. A growing permissiveness on the part of the public, the rise of what is described as the "counterculture," and an increasing skepticism of the so-called "work ethic" turned many college graduates and others away from careers in business. The decade was a period of strife and unrest. An unpopular war, the struggle of minorities to enter the mainstream of the nation's life, and perhaps the very affluence of society itself were among contributing causes to what many considered was becoming an almost anarchic situation.

All this had a tremendous impact on industry. The employees of industry are a reflection of the society in which they live, and the consequences were extremely serious. Absenteeism soared, quality of goods and services declined, and there were strikes. Labor leaders, like their industrial counterparts, frequently complained of the breakdown of discipline within their organizations, for the United States witnessed the previously rare spectacle of rank-and-file union members picketing union business offices.

But the reaction was inevitable. The pendulum swung, and with the end of the war in Vietnam, protest substantially subsided. However, this did not bring about a return to previous conditions. There had been great changes in almost every aspect of society. Consider the contemporary relationship of the employee with his employer. Today an employee does not just want a job; he wants an "interesting, challenging job." Nor is he satisfied with reasonable job security. He also wants more paid leisure in the form of longer vacations, more holidays, and a shorter workweek. No longer does he simply accept management rules regulating his behavior on the job, especially if adherence to such rules requires him to make adjustments in his hair style, mode of dress, or manner of living. In such situations he may require a company to justify a regulation that he thinks interferes with his personal freedom or rights, even if this means court action.

The changing attitude of employees toward their jobs has prompted management to experiment in new and different approaches toward motivating them. Many companies have encouraged the participation of workers in certain areas of decision making and in the establishment of their own work objectives. Some companies, also with the goal of securing greater employee job enthusiasm through greater employee participation, have installed programs of job enlargement, job rotation, and job enrichment, all designed to make work more interesting and stimulating. Certainly if you judge the overall thrust of management's contemporary personnel programs—at least so far as the articles and publicity statements about them are concerned—you immediately conclude that the proponents of "Theory Y" have at last come into their own.

The traditional view of employee relations, which Douglas McGregor called "Theory X," held that man does not like work and will avoid it if he can; that most people must be coerced, controlled, and threatened with punishment to persuade them to work; that the average person prefers to be directed, has little ambition, and wants security above all else. The modern theory, according to McGregor—"Theory Y"—emphasizes managerial leadership through motivation by objectives and by permitting subordinates to experience personal satisfaction as they contribute to achievement objectives of the company.

But it is impossible for any company to operate successfully as a debating society. There must be management. Discipline must still be applied or organization disintegrates. Douglas McGregor recognized this when, after he had served in a managerial position, he wrote:

> I believed, for example, that a leader could operate successfully as kind of advisor to his organization. I thought I could avoid being a boss. Unconsciously, I suspect, I hoped to duck the unpleasant necessity of making difficult decisions, of taking responsibility for one course of action, among many uncertain alternatives, of making mistakes and taking the consequences. I thought that I would operate so that everyone would like me— that good human relations would eliminate all discord and disagreement.

I couldn't have been more wrong. It took a couple of years, but I finally began to realize that a leader cannot avoid the exercise of authority any more than he can avoid responsibility for what happens to an organization.*

Good human relations is highly desirable, but it will not take the place of a firm, consistently fair, properly administered discipline program. And the operation of such a program is largely in the hands of the supervisor who makes his company's on-the-floor decisions about the day-to-day questions on such matters as wages, hours, and working conditions. His responsibilities are certainly more complex than they have ever been before, and to carry them out properly he must have a thorough knowledge of his firm's labor relations policies and practices, good judgment, and an understanding of the needs and motivations of his subordinates.

DISCIPLINE AND "JUST CAUSE"

Unfortunately, too many employees, and managers also, are inclined to define "discipline" in its narrow or punitive sense. "Discipline" has a far broader meaning than punishment. When a supervisor penalizes an employee for a violation of a rule or some other infraction, the penalty should be imposed not for the sake of punishment but to restore him to the order of the group.

The very word "discipline" should convey a positive meaning. The scholar is complimented when he is told he has a disciplined mind, for he has trained himself to reason in a logical and orderly manner and avoid errors of haste or carelessness. A championship athletic team or a crack military unit is generally referred to as "well disciplined" because its members work together with machinelike precision. Branches of learning are also called "disciplines" because in acquiring proficiency in one of them a student disciplines himself intellectually.

So if you think of discipline in its total meaning, you realize

* Douglas McGregor, "On Leadership," *Antioch Notes*, May 1954, pp. 2–3.

that it is the sinew of organization, the glue that holds the pieces together. Good discipline permits efficient up-and-down communications, encourages cooperation, and builds team pride. Happily the majority of people prefer to live and work in a disciplined environment. They instinctively know that fair rules are necessary for the protection of both the individual and the group, and that without them it would be impossible for people to work together. They believe that rules and regulations must be administered impartially and that the principle of "just cause" should govern the imposition of any penalty for the violation of any rule.

"Just cause" is the foundation on which the American legal system rests. It simply means that a punishment should not be in excess of the seriousness of an offense and that all circumstances (especially those which may mitigate its gravity) surrounding the offense should be considered before any penalty is affixed.

Punishment for just cause is usually accepted by employees as necessary, and fairness and consistency in the administration of discipline help make it a positive force in employee relations. Positive discipline, however, is generally self-enforcing. It underwrites a company's strength, its resiliency, and its capacity to move quickly and efficiently. It reflects the quality of organizational morale and gives direction to collective action.

Practically every union-management agreement permits a company to impose discipline on an employee for just cause. But always it is up to the individual supervisor to determine what is "just cause." Before he decides to discipline a worker, he should be able to answer these questions: (1) Is the employee guilty of the offense? (2) Are there any extenuating circumstances? (3) If the employee is guilty of the offense, to what extent should he be punished for it? (4) Has proper discipline procedure been observed in handling this case?

These last two questions are most important. For example, in deciding the extent of punishment an employee is to receive, a supervisor should consider the following factors: past practice, the employee's prior discipline record, his explanation of his action, his seniority, and any other circumstances that might mitigate the degree of punishment. Even if a supervisor carefully observes each of the foregoing items before he imposes discipline, he may still find his case shot from under him if he makes technical mistakes in administration or if he attempts, in the interest of saving time, to shortcut the established discipline procedure.

STEPS IN THE DISCIPLINE PROCEDURE

There are a series of extremely grave offenses, such as stealing, drinking on the job, bringing a dangerous weapon onto plant property, fighting, and conducting a large-scale gambling operation, that unions and companies usually agree *may* be (but are not always) a cause for immediate dismissal. But the majority of discharge cases do not come about through such dramatic circumstances. They are the result of an accumulation of minor offenses, none of which by itself merits severe punishment but which, taken all together, indicate a behavior pattern on the part of the employee that management finds intolerable.

Discipline procedures vary in detail from company to company, but generally the steps in the process are as follows:

1. *A friendly and unofficial warning by the supervisor to the offending employee.* If an employee is guilty of some minor offense, for example, too much absenteeism, excessive tardiness, and below-standard performance, a supervisor usually brings the employee's shortcoming to his attention with the suggestion that the employee had better correct his fault or expect more serious consequences if it recurs. This warning is usually not entered in the employee's official discipline record. However, it is still a good practice for the supervisor to make a dated note of the fact that he has spoken to the employee about the deficiency.

2. *The warning interview.* If an employee disregards his super-

visor's unofficial warnings, the usual discipline procedure requires a supervisor to call him in for a warning interview. Such a discussion should be private and the supervisor should provide the specifics of the employee's offenses: for example, dates, nature of offenses, and the effect his acts are having on the operation of the group. The employee should be given full opportunity to defend his actions or at least to present his side of the case and explain his reasons for failing to adhere to company discipline standards. If the supervisor judges that the employee deserves a reprimand for his acts or behavior, it should be given to the employee at the conclusion of the interview or shortly thereafter. Usually a grievance procedure requires that a written copy of an official reprimand be provided the employee, and in it the supervisor should spell out the nature of the employee's offense or offenses, the dates of occurrence, and the dates on which the supervisor informally called the employee's attention to his deficiencies and asked him to change his ways. A copy of the warning reprimand and a summary of the warning interview should be inserted in the employee's personnel file and another copy (if this is required by the union agreement) should be given to the union.

In the majority of cases a warning interview with the accompanying reprimand (if one is given) is sufficient to bring about the desired change in an employee's behavior. But the effectiveness of this step in the discipline procedure depends on the judgment of the supervisor together with his knowledge of the attitudes, motivations, and ambitions of his subordinates. If a supervisor knows his people well, he knows how they will respond to reprimands, and he acts accordingly. Certain subordinates need only to have him call attention to their mistakes. Other employees are not so easy to handle, and it may take a stern, straight-from-the-shoulder lecture to return them to cooperation and proper disciplinary habits.

3. *The disciplinary layoff.* If a warning interview and reprimand do not succeed, there is one remaining penalty short of dismissal

that a supervisor can use to correct the erring employee. It is the disciplinary layoff. This can vary anywhere from one day to several days in length, depending on the gravity of the offense. A disciplinary layoff should not be imposed unless an employee has totally ignored both friendly and official warnings and reprimands. Its objective is obvious. The enforced idleness and loss of pay force the employee to the realization that if he continues to violate plant discipline it can only result in dismissal, and not too many people are willing to jeopardize their jobs foolishly.

4. *Discharge.* Dismissal is industry's capital punishment and should be used only for extremely grave offenses or for continuous and willful violation of company rules and regulations. Discharge is a serious matter. An employee who is terminated for cause has many problems. His unemployment pay may be affected and he may find it extremely difficult to locate a new job. Arbitrators are aware of all this, and discharge cases that come to them for a hearing are likely to be closely scrutinized. Many arbitrators are inclined to reduce penalities of dismissal to lesser punishments if they can find any reasons for so doing. Therefore it is absolutely essential to make sure that proper procedure has been observed at every step of the discipline process in all discharge cases.

HOW TO MAKE SURE THE PRINCIPLES OF JUST CAUSE ARE BEING OBSERVED'

Under the grievance procedure of the normal management-union agreement, employees are protected from the unjust, capricious, or discriminatory imposition of discipline. If a worker believes that his rights have been violated, that discipline procedure has been ignored, or that the supervisor's administration of discipline has been inconsistent or unfair, he may file a grievance with the assurance that if he has a substantial case, he can take his arguments all the way to an impartial arbitrator for a final decision. Many well-run nonunion companies have also established similar procedures to safeguard the rights of their employees. However, by observing the principles outlined in the following checklist a supervisor will acquire an evenhanded objectivity in handling discipline cases that will gain him the respect and confidence of employees.

1. *Assure the privacy of all disciplinary actions.* The object in disciplining an employee is to change his behavior or correct his fault, not just to punish him. So never hold a subordinate up to public ridicule through a public rebuke. Keep all discipline discussions private—between you and the offender.

2. *Be prompt.* If a penalty is deserved, it should be swiftly imposed. If there is too long a delay between the offense and its punishment, the penalty loses its effectiveness. The employee tends to forget what he has done and remembers only his punishment. Of course, you should not be overhasty in decision making or act impulsively or unfairly in the administration of discipline. But bear in mind that the longer a supervisor keeps an employee waiting for the imposition of a punishment, the more the latter tends to think the penalty—whatever it is—is not merited.

3. *Be consistent but not rigidly so.* Every discipline case must be judged on the facts surrounding it. A code of penalties for offenses should never be imposed so narrowly that a particular punishment is unfair to an employee. Extenuating circumstances and an employee's past record should always be considered.

4. *Avoid entrapment.* Never try to force a trouble-making employee into a position which provokes him into an act of insubordination and provides you with an excuse to terminate him. The chances are that this gambit will not work anyhow. If the employee or his union can prove that you entrapped the former into insubordination by your contributory act, your decision is likely to be reversed.

5. *Keep good records.* Inadequate records are a major reason why supervisors are frequently unable to justify discipline de-

cisions. Your records should contain the facts you will need if you are ever called upon to justify a discipline penalty at a higher level of the grievance procedure or at arbitration.

6. *Avoid double jeopardy.* You cannot punish a man twice for the same offense. Once a penalty has been imposed, the case is closed. You cannot add to the penalty later even if additional evidence comes to light that shows that the employee is even more deserving of punishment than you originally thought.

7. *Follow precedent.* Past practice is important. If you penalize an employee for acts other employees have committed without being punished or for which they have received lesser penalties, an arbitrator will think your penalty is excessive and reduce or reverse it.

8. *Do not use demotion as a punishment.* You may downgrade an employee for failing to meet job requirements or if there is an economic cutback which means a reduction in force. But you should not demote him for purely disciplinary reasons. Nor is it wise to try to do so by making the superficial claim that you are demoting a worker for poor work when your real reason is punishment. Unless your records show frequent warnings and even disciplinary actions for poor work, it is not very likely that your ruse will work.

9. *Restore the normal relationship with the employee as quickly as possible after punishment.* Make sure he realizes the book is closed on his past and that you bear him no grudges. Your attitude should be friendly, and the employee should realize that your job is to help him and not to play policeman.

THE SUPERVISOR AND THE ADMINISTRATION OF DISCIPLINE

The supervisor is essential to the effective administration of discipline. By sound leadership he can do much to create a working climate in which the enforcement of discipline is a natural process because employees accept and observe rules and policies as normal safeguards to their job success and personal welfare. However, there are certain difficulties that confront the modern supervisor.

For one thing, labor turnover is high. "How do we get and retain good people?" is a question constantly on management's mind. Many employees, well aware that their skills have high market value, change jobs much more frequently than was formerly the case.

For another, many marginal employees have entered the work force. Fair employment laws and the high demand for workers are among the reasons why management has lowered its selection standards. Today many applicants are hired who a decade previously would not have been considered proper job candidates except for the most unskilled laboring jobs. Such employees often require extensive and lengthy training before they can become acceptable producers.

In addition, unions have become more aggressive. Inflation has eaten away at the purchasing power of the dollar. The reaction of employees has been to demand that their unions press hard for increases that will keep their wages in line with living costs. Unions are themselves political and highly competitive. If one union wins a large and widely publicized settlement from a major industry, that settlement, or perhaps one even more attractive, becomes the goal of other unions. For the leaders of any union know that if they fail to convince members that they are giving them full value for dues money, the union is in deep trouble.

Inflation is not the only reason for labor's aggressiveness. The modern union member is as quick to criticize and challenge what he considers weak or complacent union leadership as he is to find fault with management, and he expects his union to get him his share of the economic pie. Minorities too are looking closely and critically at the leadership of their unions. Often they suspect that they are not getting their share of union offices or that they are not being represented properly at grievance hearings. Should their suspicions ever become a conviction, the leadership of the union can look for nothing but trouble. Labor has always had reasons to be aggressive at the bargaining table and when speaking for its members in disputes with management. But today in view of the severe internal difficulties many unions are having in adjusting conflicts of interest between various groups in their own memberships, labor leaders know that the best way to divert the attention of members from internal problems is to direct it toward management, and that the aggressive pursuit of union goals is the best form of protection from member dissatisfaction that a union can have.

To live up to his responsibilities, a supervisor must understand some basic facts about the administration of discipline. They are:

1. *Sound training leads to sound discipline.* One meaning of the word "discipline" is to instruct others and help them acquire the knowledge and skill necessary to do a particular job. The supervisor who wants a disciplined work force cannot neglect training. Badly trained employees are unhappy, frustrated, and undisciplined.

2. *Discipline cannot exist without good controls.* The supervisor must have the control system he needs to direct his subordinates properly. This means that he must personally follow up, use written or oral communications (such as reports), and keep himself accurately informed on the activities of his department. A sure way to destroy discipline is to permit employees to get the idea that the boss does not know (or does not care) what is going on.

3. *Effective communications is the foundation of positive discipline.* To assure good discipline there must be quick, two-way communications between a boss and his subordinates. To be a successful communicator a supervisor should be perceptive, alert to the attitudes, needs, and ambitions of employees, and ready to give them help and advice on job-related problems. Employees have a right to be kept informed on matters affecting their jobs

or working conditions, and if a supervisor wants to make sure that rules, policies, and performance standards are observed, he must take the time and trouble to explain them and to help workers understand that these stipulations are both fair and necessary to the proper functioning of the department.

But even the best organization, if not carefully maintained and properly adjusted periodically to meet changing conditions, will soon begin to show signs of stress and deterioration. A decline in positive discipline is, perhaps, the most telling symptom that all is not organizationally right and that quick remedial steps are necessary to restore organizational efficiency.

SIGNS OF DISCIPLINARY TROUBLES

What are the signs of coming disciplinary problems? Most are self-evident, but employee attitude is the key. If employees, for whatever reason, lose confidence in their leadership and in their organization, they become uncertain and frustrated, possibly even angry, and their feelings may be evidenced by their actions. So if you observe a rise in absenteeism, tardiness, grievances (real or imaginary), sullenness sometimes (if matters are not corrected) amounting almost to insubordination, and a decline in the productivity and quality of goods and services, you are facing a disciplinary dilemma, and quick constructive action to return the situation to your control is absolutely essential.

Some of the reasons for such disciplinary problems may be beyond your power to correct, particularly if they are widespread throughout the organization. But any capable supervisor can certainly do a great deal to avoid difficulties if he is an effective and fair administrator and if he provides his subordinates with that brand of constructive leadership that minimizes disciplinary troubles.

When a supervisor senses that subordinates are disturbed and unhappy about some yet unidentified problem, he should immediately investigate to discover its nature and dimensions. If he finds that the problem is of a kind that he can do something about himself, by taking quick corrective steps he may ward off later unpleasantness. If it is due to circumstances over which he has no control, he should inform his management in time for intelligent preventive measures to be taken.

A review of the various signs of disciplinary problems, their causes, and what to do about them may be useful in the administration of positive discipline.

Absenteeism

Absenteeism and tardiness are closely related. In fact, the only real difference between the employee who is late and the one who is absent is one of degree; the first is absent only part of the day while the other misses work altogether. Neither is a help to organizational efficiency or productivity.

Of course, everybody is absent or tardy occasionally, usually with good reason. This is normal and does not in any way constitute a disciplinary problem. However, if absenteeism or tardiness in your department begins to climb above its usual average, it is well to find out why as rapidly as you can in order to bring the situation back under control.

While there may be no simple solution to the problem, experts say that the relationship between the supervisor and employees, the importance an employee places on his work, and his interest in doing it are certainly factors affecting his attendance. Regardless of the kind of job a person holds, his enthusiasm for getting to work every day is closely related to his desire to do the job itself. Absenteeism is also influenced by the leadership the supervisor provides, the morale and attitude of the work group, and the feeling on the part of the employee that his effort is both recognized and appreciated by his boss and that his absence will be noticed and will lessen team effectiveness.

Credit and recognition for good attendance are important. A high absentee rate becomes more understandable if certain groups of employees assigned to monotonous, repetitive jobs get the idea that their work is so routine that whether a particular individual is absent is a matter of indifference to the supervisor and that if someone is willing to miss a day's pay along with missing the day itself, who is losing anything?

However, absenteeism is a serious problem, and industry's bill for it is costly. A company president listed the following dollar items that can be directly attributed to high absenteeism.

1. Interrupted schedules, production slowdowns, and customer inconvenience.

2. Increased training costs.

3. More and unneeded overtime pay.

4. Higher waste and greater inefficiency that can be traced to substitutes doing jobs for which they lack experience, are untrained, or are out of practice.

5. Unneeded employees on the payroll serving as back-ups for frequently absent workers.

While reprimand, layoff, or termination may be the only method of dealing with the habitual absentee, the experienced leader relies on punishment only when all other means of positive motivation have failed. The best way to keep a tight rein on absenteeism is through a sound system of controls and the self-disciplined example of management itself. Managerial laxity in the enforcement of rules has an unhappy effect on employee attitudes and a negative influence on attendance. However, if regulations on absenteeism are applied consistently and a supervisor fulfills his accountability as a fair and consistent administrator of discipline, absenteeism on a wide scale is not so likely to occur.

The following checklist may help establish sound absentee controls and assist you in keeping a checkrein on absenteeism:

1. *Be aware of the importance of absentee control.* High employee morale is reflected by high attendance. When an employee

is missing from action even for a day, say something about it to let him know you missed him. If he has been sick, ask how he is feeling; if his absence was due to some other reason, find out whether he has resolved the situation. Your friendly concern about his welfare is appreciated. Telephone or visit ill employees, and when they return to work, go out of your way to let them know you are glad to have them back and that they have been missed by you and their associates.

2. *Make sure your records are accurate.* They are important in absentee control. By studying them you can identify that small group of employees who usually run up your absentee rate and you can take proper measures to prevent the practice from continuing.

3. *Train thoroughly.* Good training is an antidote to absenteeism. Frequent absence not only denotes low morale but is sometimes a sign of poor supervisory leadership. Badly trained workers are frustrated and unhappy on jobs which they perform poorly and are likely to express their discontent by taking unscheduled holidays whenever they feel like it. However, competent employees whose job performance shows thorough training are self-confident, efficient, and seldom missing.

4. *Be consistent in enforcement of rules.* Management that is alternately lax and severe creates its own disciplinary problems, including high absenteeism. Apply the rules governing absenteeism with intelligent consistency, always remembering that the best method of controlling such a problem is to build proper employee attitudes which encourage people to come to work because they want to, not because they are afraid that staying home will bring reprisal.

5. *Make sure employees understand at the beginning that high absenteeism will not be permitted.* Firmness is your only response to the chronic absentee. Positive methods of motivation are the most effective tools of absentee control for most people, but they must be backed up by fair discipline and by prompt rule enforce-

ment should an employee (or group of employees) habitually stay away from the job.

Tardiness

While the cause of a high rate of absenteeism may be poor supervision, lack of motivation, inferior working conditions, or dissatisfaction with monotonous or repetitive jobs, tardiness (especially if unaccompanied by a high absentee rate) is almost always a sign of indifferent management leadership. Supervision simply refuses to worry if employees report a few minutes late. Practically every company has a rule insisting on the punctuality of personnel (including managers). But all too often very little is done to enforce such rules, particularly if a late comer misses the starting hour by only a few minutes. As a matter of fact, managers and supervisors themselves do not always set good examples in promptness. Time clocks do offer an automatic deterrent to tardiness in that they require that employees "punch in" before starting or be docked fractionally for working time lost. But such a monetary loss may not be too much if the employee is "almost on time" and his worry about it is proportionately small.

However, employee tardiness does not necessarily mean that employees are dissatisfied with their jobs or with their leadership. It might reveal that management itself is to blame for not insisting that its members run a taut ship.

Tardiness is all too frequent (and expensive) to be disregarded as not of pressing importance. Therefore the question might very well be asked, "Why are people late?" The answer comes in three parts: (1) accidental causes—factors beyond employee control, for example, highway traffic jam, breakdowns; (2) employee to blame —too big a weekend, oversleeping, faulty alarm clock; (3) supervisor responsible—management laxity, that is, failure to enforce rules.

You cannot do anything to cut down tardiness caused by circumstances beyond an employee's control and you have no reason to doubt his word unless his attendance record is bad and he is an expert at alibis. But you can certainly reduce the rate of tardiness due to the other two causes. To do this you require a sound system of controls plus attendance standards that are understood and accepted by employees and enforced by you. Here are some ideas that have been proven successful in reducing tardiness.

1. *Do not shrug off tardiness.* Consistent and completely fair application of the company's rules governing tardiness is an important control mechanism. Of course, you must use judgment. If penalties become so severe that an employee, fearing to be late, prefers to stay home with the excuse that he is sick rather than face punishment or a lecture, your approach is self-defeating. However, a late comer should realize that his tardiness has been observed and that he is not getting away with anything. Ask him, "Why?" If his lateness is repeated, make sure he understands that his dilatoriness is hurting group effort, and that you must insist he observe punctuality standards.

2. *Make sure employees understand rules.* Do not take it for granted that simply because they have been listed in the handbooks or posted on the bulletin board, rules are understood. Use communications in training to build the importance of punctuality (and good attendance). Let it be unmistakably known that excessive tardiness, just like habitual absenteeism, will have unpleasant consequences. You do not have to harp on the possibility of punishment to get this point across. But you do have to let employees know that you expect them to obey the rules just as you do.

3. *Show appreciation for outstanding attendance and punctuality.* The punctual, dependable employee deserves your recognition and should know that his effort has not passed unnoticed— or unappreciated. Your gratitude encourages him to continue and is a spur to all employees to come to work regularly and on time.

4. *Keep an eye on the habitually late arrival.* Good records en-

able you to identify people who cause most of your tardiness problem. Tell the chronic laggard frankly that punctuality is an essential job requirement. Explain why, from the standpoint of group efficiency, it is essential for him to correct his fault. Ask him to identify the causes of his lateness and tell you what he will do to improve his record.

5. *Emphasize the essentiality of each individual to the organization.* Assure each subordinate that you consider both him and his work absolutely necessary to the accomplishment of the group. Encourage employees to discuss problems with you, and seek their ideas and suggestions. If a person realizes that his absence or lateness undermines the operation of the team, he usually does his best to be on time.

6. *Lead by example.* You cannot expect punctuality in others unless you are punctual yourself. If you stroll in late, you cannot blame employees if they are not too concerned about being late themselves. If you are too busy with other matters to worry about punctuality in subordinates, they will assume you are not too upset if they are tardy.

INSUBORDINATION

Insubordination is perhaps the most serious challenge to management discipline that a supervisor encounters. It is a direct and provocative challenge to authority. Usually acts of insubordination are limited to one or a few employees. If it is on a large scale, it becomes evident in such activities as the sit-down or wildcat strike.

The majority of companies have rules that plainly say that an act of insubordination, such as refusing to obey the reasonable orders of a superior, may be a cause for immediate termination, and unions have never seriously challenged the need for such regulations. However, an individual act of insubordination must be treated on its own merits and the supervisor must decide what to do about it with calm and deliberate judgment. Often what may appear on the surface to be a case of insubordination is not that at all, and a union, in defending an employee so charged, will claim "mitigating circumstances," that "procedure was not properly followed," or that "the employee was entrapped," and either clear the offender completely or succeed in having his penalty reduced.

There are three basic types of insubordination:

1. *An employee deliberately challenges the authority of his superior and intends a showdown.* Occasionally a person who dislikes his boss and believes he has the support of his group (or his union) will start an argument to demonstrate his power or the supervisor's lack of it. There are many arbitration cases which describe situations of this kind.

2. *The employee loses his temper and his self-control.* For some reason, possibly because he thinks he is being unfairly treated, a subordinate gets into a blazing argument with his superior. His judgment deserts him, and in such a mood he may be guilty of what is technically insubordination.

3. *Entrapment.* A supervisor, because of animosity toward an employee or for some other reason, desires to terminate him but can find no legitimate reason to do so. He purposely provokes the employee and traps him into an argument in order to penalize or even dismiss him. Such a practice is rare, as the well-trained supervisory of today would hardly resort to a strategy that is unfair and has little chance of success. He knows that arbitrators look hard at any case of alleged insubordination to make sure that entrapment is not an element.

If you are confronted with individual acts of insubordination, there are certain tried and proven rules that you should follow in coping with the problem. They are as follows:

1. *Make certain any order you give is entirely reasonable.* Under certain conditions an employee may have the right to refuse to obey an order that he considers unreasonable. Such orders might include doing hazardous work or doing an assignment out of his job classification. From the employee's point of view it is safer to

carry out the order and file a grievance afterward. Refusal to obey an order on the grounds it is unreasonable or the supervisor lacks authority to give it means he is substituting his judgment for that of his boss, and he may be wrong—and insubordinate. Nevertheless, if a worker argues that an order is unreasonable and is reluctant to obey, do not be hasty in declaring him insubordinate. Before you demand that he execute your instructions, check to be sure that the work is in his job classification, that it is reasonably safe, and that he has the ability and experience to do it. If you are asking him to do unusual work because of an emergency, make certain you have a true emergency and are not creating one to get him to do a job he ordinarily would not have to do.

2. *Be sure there is no misunderstanding.* There are times when a worker's failure to do a job or to perform it properly is due to failure in communications. The badly done job or the occurrence of a job not done at all may so enrage a supervisor that he decides the employee's offense was deliberate. You cannot afford to lose your temper. A good leader must practice self-control. Before you penalize an employee for insubordination, be absolutely certain that he has understood what you wanted him to do, that he was qualified to do it, and that his refusal to comply really was insubordination. In giving instructions, do not take chances. If you have the slightest doubt as to whether an employee understands your orders, go over the assignment with him again and check up later to see that it is being done right.

3. *Follow procedure.* Do not take shortcuts. Policies, rules, and procedures governing the administration of discipline should be strictly observed, especially in insubordination cases.

4. *Do not accept hearsay or unchecked evidence.* Investigate carefully and make sure any information that you plan to introduce to sustain a charge of insubordination is reliable. Hasty or impulsive decisions are not likely to stand up. They will be reversed either by higher management or by an arbitrator, and this does not make you look good.

5. *Make sure the charge is the correct one.* Accuracy is all-

important. Never use an accusation of insubordination as a general indictment because you cannot determine exactly what an employee's offense is. For example, a subordinate who is generally a substandard performer or who has a bad attitude should not be penalized for insubordination because it is too much trouble to frame a more precise indictment. When you claim that someone has been insubordinate, you must back your specifics by facts. You should be able to explain what the offender did, what he said, and in what circumstances. An arbitrator may be looking at your decision with a critical eye.

6. *Avoid entrapment.* Be certain your own record is perfectly clear and can bear close examination. Never become involved in any act that may bring about the counter-allegation of entrapment. If the employee can prove that your words or actions contributed to his offense, he will probably get his penalty set aside.

7. *Investigate causes.* You cannot tolerate insubordination and still maintain management authority. But the act of insubordination has a serious meaning above and beyond the offense of the employee. By challenging his supervisor a person is also communicating, protesting some situation which he believes is so unjust or discriminatory that he is willing to put his job on the line to correct matters. True, he may have no legitimate case—he may simply be a troublemaker. On the other hand he may be telling the supervisor that high-handed methods are incurring great resentment, so much so that he finally decided to take action even at the risk of termination. After handling cases of insubordination it is wise to examine your own managerial and leadership methods to make sure they are fair and that you are doing your best to be consistent and objective in the administration of discipline.

ILLEGAL WORK STOPPAGES

The wildcat strike and related work stoppages such as sit-down strikes and slowdowns are illegal, are usually conducted in violation of a union contract and of established procedures, and are instances of what might be described as mass insubordination—not only against management but perhaps against the authority of a union itself. A company has the right to terminate anyone participating, but the strikers usually rely on their number to prevent this kind of retribution.

Final strategy and action decisions on how to handle this type of trouble must be made by top management. But a supervisor can be of immense help in making sure that his superiors come up with the right decision by providing them with fast, accurate information on events as they develop. He is on the scene and is the best source of facts regarding the causes and course of the incident. He must keep his head, stay on the floor, and simultaneously get the news to higher management as quickly as he can. Because he must stay at his post, the telephone and written or oral messages are his usual means of communications.

The supervisor should also warn employees of what may happen to them if they take part in an illegal work stoppage and should certainly do his best to identify its ringleaders. If employees engage in a sit-down strike instead of walking out, the supervisor should give them orders to perform normal tasks and note the names of all persons who refuse to obey instructions. But he should never given an option to an employee about doing his work, for example, "Either do the job or leave the plant." If he makes such a mistake, the employee may claim later that he went home because he had his boss's permission to do so.

Authorities in industrial relations suggest the following guides for handling wildcats, slowdowns, sit-downs, and similar types of mass disciplinary breakdowns.

1. *Be on the alert for danger signals.* A perceptive supervisor quickly detects changes in employee moods, attitudes, and habits. If employees are frustrated, their feelings may reveal themselves in sudden rashes of complaints and grievances (many perhaps manufactured), and their behavior pattern alters. Upward communications may wither away and employees who were formerly

open and free with their opinions and ideas become reserved and laconic. The actions and attitude of the shop steward are also a barometer of the climate. If he becomes hostile and aggressive, magnifying and building each little issue into a major dispute, storm warnings are flying. A supervisor should try to discover the causes of the trouble and quickly relay information on what is happening to higher management. They may be able to take sensible steps to adjust the situation.

2. *Check on types of grievances being submitted.* A supervisor expects a certain number of grievances and can usually settle them promptly. Grievances in themselves usually offer no special problem. But if there is an unexpected flood of them all revolving around one or two related issues that hitherto have been of minor consequence, they may indicate a future union bargaining demand. A supervisor is hardly able to settle grievances of this nature. The union does not want them settled. But he should know that as a matter of long-range strategy unions occasionally resort to tactics of this kind to harass a company and occasionally may even give covert support to a wildcat strike or other forms of labor disruption to wear down management and weaken its resistance to an upcoming demand. Top executives (especially those dealing with labor relations) need full information on such matters in order to develop management's counter strategy.

3. *Be familiar with the political situation inside a union.* Some wildcat strikes are led by people who aspire to union power. Such a person may consider present union leadership weak and vacillating and ready to be replaced. A natural leader of this kind may persuade a group of employees that it is too time-consuming, chancy, and tedious to use the grievance procedure to settle a complaint or the bargaining table to negotiate a demand, and that direct action is the best way to attain an objective. The potential leader of a wildcat strike may even be a minor officer of his own union, ambitious for power, or possibly the advance agent of a rival union which hopes to replace the incumbent one. This kind

of trouble-making employee must be identified. A fomenter of unrest is a constant threat to operational stability.

4. *Try to identify leaders of illegal work stoppages.* A company can seldom terminate everyone participating in an unlawful work stoppage, especially if it involves a number of people. That is what its leaders are counting on—safety in numbers. However, if you can identify the leaders and substantiate the identification with proof, you can have them punished. They triggered the action and bear the greatest responsibility. Decisions of arbitrators usually support management for penalizing such people when it can definitely prove they were the instigators. A supervisor is his company's on-the-spot observer, and it is up to him to name names as to who did what and when and to back his accusations with facts, such as the written statements or testimony of witnesses or a written diary of events.

5. *Be certain employees know the consequences of taking part in an illegal strike.* A wildcat strike, a sit-down, and a slowdown are illegal work stoppages and generally in direct violation of a union contract. Employees should be under no misapprehension as to the penalties they may face should they be party to such action. Leaders should be informed that their union and they themselves may face legal action, and everyone involved should be told in no uncertain words that they are bypassing the grievance procedure agreed to by their own union to settle arguments taking place during the life of the contract.

6. *Strive for a prompt return to normal conditions when the strike is over.* Management cannot afford to hold grudges against employees and neither can a supervisor. Do not reveal by word, gesture, or attitude that you are still angry with certain of your subordinates and that you are just waiting for a chance to even the score. If your hostility shows, you will inadvertently be giving past offenders grounds for belief that they were completely right in doing as they did. A supervisor must work closely with his people —all of them—if he hopes to maintain a climate of positive dis-

cipline. After a labor dispute the quicker he can return working conditions to normal, the better it is immediately and the stronger the safeguard he builds against future trouble of a similar nature.

CONCLUSION

Fortunately, major problems of discipline in the average plant are the exception—not the rule. The steps you take to return the offending employee to the order of the group are standard and largely sequential: the warning, the reprimand, penalties such as layoffs, and lastly, when all else fails, termination. The average employee rarely experiences the negative aspects of discipline, and even when a punitive measure is applied, the penalty is likely to be a warning or a reprimand. Only occasionally does someone commit an offense that makes his behavior so intolerable that he is discharged.

The large majority of supervisors and managers at all levels try to use positive methods to train and motivate employees, and as a rule the typical employee is reasonably satisfied with his job if he works where his ability and work are recognized and appreciated by superiors and where he is accepted and respected by his fellow workers. To him the rules regulating job practices and conduct seem fair and necessary, and experience has taught him that his own self-discipline will enable him to work without friction with either his colleagues or his boss. He also knows that it rewards him by greater opportunity to develop his abilities, a better chance for advancement, and eventually higher monetary returns.

However, there are always some people who are not team players. Despite their individual ability, intelligence, or talents, they simply cannot or will not work within an organization without causing trouble. The kind of person who does not fit into the group and cannot be persuaded by either friendly or punitive means to do so must be removed from it. Not to be confused or lumped with the disciplinary troubles discussed above are special disciplinary problems involving disadvantaged employees, many of which can be avoided by special training. These problems are discussed in the section "Special training for the disadvantaged" at the end of Chapter 4.

The late Dr. Elliott Janney, a noted management consultant, advised:

> An executive or supervisor who can't discipline himself, can't discipline others. The employee who is undisciplined will fail on the job that demands the cooperation of others because it is simply not in his nature to give cooperation himself. No organization is big enough to hold an undisciplined person, whether worker or boss, without paying a prohibitively high price for the trouble he causes.*

It is your job to enforce all company rules and regulations fairly, objectively, and in a way to make them understood. The responsibility for maintaining discipline is yours. Nor can the challenge of the responsibility be rejected with impunity. For the reverse side of the coin of good discipline is anarchy, and the results of anarchy are catastrophic for employees, for management, and for democratic society itself.

* From the author's notebook of comments of executives in industry who participated in the author's seminars.

SEVEN

How to Administer
a Grievance Program Properly

The employee's complaint or, if the company has relations with a union, his grievance, is an important form of upward communications that should receive prompt attention and skillful handling. The employee is sending management a message. Some situation affecting his wages, hours, or working conditions has made him angry, fearful, or unhappy, and he is asking for relief or for an adjustment in a matter that he thinks is unfair or discriminatory. Whether or not the complaint has substance, the employee is entitled to a considerate hearing and should receive an explanation of the reasons for management's decision regarding it. Unsettled or unsatisfactorily adjusted complaints or grievances are a straight road to severe troubles in labor relations.

THE SUPERVISOR: KEY MAN IN
GRIEVANCE HANDLING

Who is initially responsible for the adjustment of complaints or grievances? That's right! You are! The first-line supervisor is his company's on-the-floor representative, and it is to him that employees come with their worries, their complaints, and their formal grievances. He hears their stories and makes decisions on what to do about them. He must be doing a very good job, for surveys show that between 80 and 90 percent of all formal grievances are satisfactorily handled by the supervisor at the first step of the grievance procedure. And that is a high average in anybody's league.

Modern management is well aware of the key role that supervisors play in the day-to-day administration of a company's labor relations program. That is why supervisory training programs stress such subjects as grievance handling, contract administration, the administration of discipline, the importance of policy and precedent in labor relations, and other details that a supervisor must understand and administer properly if he is to meet the responsibilities of his job. He is where the action is, at the focal point—sometimes called on to make instant and pressure decisions based on his interpretations of company policies and the union contract. He must apply the provisions of the union agreement and the rules and regulations of the company fairly and consistently to assure a proper climate of labor relations. His knowledge, judgment, and skill determine whether or not operating practice is an accurate reflection of company policy and of the intent of the union agreement.

This last is highly important. For, briefly described, a union-management agreement is nothing more or less than a mutually acceptable personnel policy handbook, reached through the collective bargaining procedure and spelling out the rights of the company, the rights of the employees, the processes that will govern the administration of the grievance machinery, the application of rules and regulations, and other items affecting the wages, hours, and working conditions of employees. But until these policies are put into practice, they are only intentions.

The difference between "what we say we will do" and "what is actually done" can be very great indeed. In labor relations, as in everything else, good intentions are the paving stones to a well-known destination in the nether regions. We are judged by our acts and not by our policies. In short, policy statements, and this certainly applies to the provisions of the union contract, are simply collections of words until they are interpreted and acted upon by supervisors. The results of the aggregate acts of supervision become operating practice—considered by arbitrators as management's official interpretation of policy.

For these reasons it is most important for supervisors to have a common understanding of the provisions of the union agreement and to give them consistent interpretation. Their decisions may become precedent, and arbitrators in deciding a dispute are inclined to consider precedent and practice much more than the language of a contract.

Management has learned this hard fact to its sorrow. It has often seen certain important rights, secured after long days of tedious bargaining, lost irretrievably because the company simply failed to use those rights at the operating level.

"More management rights have been lost through careless and lazy administration," complained a harassed labor relations executive, "than were ever lost in negotiation."

George Piccoli, director of industrial relations for GAF, Inc., made this point when he said at a supervisory conference:

> It is not the language of the agreement that is significant, it is what the supervisor understands that language to mean. Experts may negotiate the contract. But they don't administer it. That's the job of the supervisor and if he does it inefficiently, inconsistently and haphazardly, the best agreement ever written will be of little value to the company.

> Supervisory decisions become practice, and it is the supervisor who has the responsibility for making on-the-spot decisions on employee problems. These decisions frequently require him to come up with quick interpretations of the agreement. Therefore it is important for each supervisor to have a precise understanding

of what each contract clause means and how it should be applied. If he has this knowledge he builds consistency into labor relations, which is simply another way of saying that he is a top-notch administrator.*

A union agreement is at best merely a guide, not a set of instructions providing infallible answers on the proper course of action to take in every conceivable situation. It is subject to interpretation, and it is apparent what trouble would ensue if every manager were perfectly free to make his own interpretation of it. Alert companies give much attention in supervisory training to explaining the intent of the various provisions of their agreements and providing advice to supervisors on how such provisions should be interpreted and applied. Still, on many occasions you must rely on your own judgment, so it is important to keep yourself informed on precedent and practice. When you are trying to come up with the right answer to a hard question in labor relations, the more knowledge you have on how similar questions have been answered in the past, the easier it will be for you to resolve it satisfactorily. Such knowledge gives consistency to both your decisions and your actions and thus assures operating smoothness.

CATEGORIES OF GRIEVANCES

Considering the tremendous number of grievances that come to management's official attention every year, it is surprising that the categories into which they can be divided are relatively few. By and large, employee complaints center around a small number of issues—matters which directly affect employees, their jobs, or their security. You will also find that the nature of these grievances seldom changes. The same types of disputes occur (only there may be more of them) when a company is experiencing labor trouble and threatened by a work stoppage that occur when the climate

* George Piccoli, University of South Carolina management seminar, Ocean Forest Hotel, Myrtle Beach, S.C., June, 1970.

of employee relations is generally excellent. Most complaints and grievances involve one or more of the following problems.

1. *Discipline.* Grievances submitted by employees penalized for some offenses are frequent. They usually allege discrimination, supervisory failure to follow proper procedure, the imposition of excessive punishment, or a violation of the union contract.

2. *Dismissals.* Termination of employment is a continuous source of grievances. A dismissal might well come under the classification of discipline, but because of the finality of the act and because there is the greater likelihood that a grievance will occur from its imposition than from a lesser penalty, it deserves a special category. Since discharge is tantamount to capital punishment career-wise, if an employee can find any reason to get it set aside or modified, there is a good chance that he will try to do so. Arguments to void or reduce a discharge penalty generally are based on contentions of supervisory discrimination, entrapment, failure to follow procedure, or excessive punishment. If arbitrators can find any justification for requiring management to modify such punishment, they are inclined to accept the arguments.

3. *Job classifications.* Job classifications, especially if they are narrow or tight, are a frequent source of grievances. In such situations employees may complain that they have been required to do work that falls outside of their regular duties or that other employees have performed tasks that contractually belong to them; for example, a maintenance worker may file a grievance because an operator or a supervisor in the interest of saving time has made a simple repair on a machine. Narrow job classifications can be a great impediment to productivity and a source of constant trouble to a supervisor, who in order to avoid complaints must exercise extreme care and judgment in assigning work.

Another type of grievance arising out of job classifications comes from the complaint of an employee (or union) that management has rated a job too low—that the job deserves to be in a higher classification. Grievances of this nature usually occur whenever a company installs job rating or, if a job rating plan exists, when the content of a job is changed by the introduction of new methods, new techniques, or new machinery. In the latter case a grievant will usually claim that the changed content of the job entitles it to a higher classification. However, if management attempts to downgrade a job and put it in a lower classification because certain duties have been removed from it or improved technology has made it easier, the supervisor concerned can almost be sure that he will receive grievances protesting the action.

4. *Merit rating.* Companies whose compensation system for hourly employees includes merit review of employee performance to determine whether or not particular employees will receive pay raises are likely to get complaints from workers who failed to get such increases. To get around some of these complaints many managements stipulate in their union contracts that all employees who meet minimal job standards will automatically advance to the midpoint of the rate ranges for their jobs, but that thereafter their pay raises will be based either wholly or partially on performance. Obviously it is up to the supervisor to judge the quality of a worker's performance, and if he decides after reviewing it that a worker is undeserving of a raise, that raise will not be forthcoming. The employee, however, may disagree with his supervisor's decision and file a grievance complaining that he has been unfairly treated. In such an event it is up to the supervisor to justify his decision, and this means that he may be called upon to produce records (production, safety, housekeeping, attendance, discipline, etc.) to show that his denial of an increase to the worker was based on a sound, objective review of his performance and was in no way discriminatory.

5. *Overtime.* The distribution of overtime is a cause of many grievances. Charges that because of favoritism or for some other discriminatory reason an employee did not get his fair share of overtime hours, that he missed his rightful turn in the rotation of

overtime, that he did not receive overtime work for which he was qualified by job classification and experience, are constantly heard in grievance cases.

6. *Seniority.* You can expect grievances when you must make decisions regarding promotions, transfers, and demotions, especially if you use both "ability" and "seniority" as your criteria. For example, if you award a promotion to a junior employee on the grounds that he is better qualified to perform the higher-rated jobs than is a senior employee in the same job classification, you should be prepared to defend and justify your decision with documentary evidence such as production records, attendance records, and discipline records.

7. *Work assignments.* Many grievances are the result of employee claims that they have not been treated fairly in the assignment of jobs. The employees argue that the supervisor involved played favorites and gave the easy jobs to friends, while they were left to do the unpleasant ones.

DISCOVER THE CAUSES

If you can distinguish the real cause of a grievance from its surface look, you have found the key to the mastery of labor relations problems. The thing to do is to develop a systematic approach to grievance analysis. It will enable you to look at the total pattern of grievances, see how one relates to another, and quickly tell if an undue amount of grievances stems from essentially the same causes. The following suggested steps may be helpful.

1. *Examine the grievance as a whole.* What is its relationship to other grievances? Is it admissible under the grievance procedure, or is it merely an expression of the unhappiness or frustration of the grievant?

2. *Make a part-by-part study of the grievance.* Answer such questions as: What conditions were the cause of the employee

complaint? Were they job-related? Does his complaint express the employee's real dissatisfaction or is it merely a mirror reflecting his general discontent?

3. *Relate the grievance to the person.* Do you normally have good relations with the employee? Does he have domestic or off-the-job problems that might influence his attitude? Does he get along with other workers? Is there any reason not expressed in the grievance that might be making him feel insecure or unhappy; for example, failure to get a merit increase? a transfer? a promotion? Such factors certainly have an effect on an employee's attitude and may cause him to look for fancied wrongs and to be grievance-prone.

4. *What is the general attitude of the employee?* Is he highly motivated? Or is he a marginal performer? What is his record? Perhaps he is a chronic griper? He may also be seeking political power in the union and believe that he can impress his associates by standing up for his rights and refusing to let management push him around. You can never get to the real cause of a grievance without knowing a good bit about the kind of person who has submitted it.

A SUPERVISOR'S GUIDE TO THE ADMINISTRATION OF THE GRIEVANCE PROCEDURE

Since the acts of the supervisor are so often used as the grounds on which employees base their arguments in grievance hearings, you can see why sound judgment is needed to handle grievances properly. A supervisor must consider what is fair to the employee, the other employees, and the company. He must be certain that the extent of the penalty is in line with the gravity of the act. This means he must weigh such facts as the employee's past disciplinary record, his seniority, and the seriousness of what he did, and must determine what, if any, mitigating circumstances should be taken into account. Furthermore, the discipline procedure as described in the union agreement must be observed to assure the employee the full protection of his rights. Otherwise decisions may be reversed later by superiors on technical grounds.

However, when the supervisor is finally ready to decide what to do, he must still make judgment decisions, for there are likely to be differences of opinion on any decision affecting a particular disciplinary case. But so long as he confines such disagreements to "opinions" and his acts do not go counter to normal company policy or practice, there will be reasonable uniformity in contract administration. Such consistency is the foundation of sound labor relations and a positive approach to the handling of grievances.

The following guide may be helpful.

1. *Define the grievance.* Find out from the employee the exact nature of his complaint before taking any action. To do so you must pay full attention to his story, and perhaps use questions to dig for the real problem. Possibly when you discover precisely what the employee is griping about, you will see that he does not have a real grievance—at least, one that under the terms of the union agreement entitles him to file a formal complaint. Nevertheless, if ignored, a grievance, real or fancied, can cause difficulties. If a worker's complaint is one you can do something about, he will appreciate your help. If not, tell him plainly why his problem is one which the company cannot solve for him. The opportunity you have given him to discuss his troubles, together with the sympathy you have shown, will probably help clear the air.

2. *Be a sympathetic listener.* The ability to listen serves a supervisor well, especially in grievance handling. A willingness to hear out an employee may take time, but it is worthwhile. Sometimes a subordinate who thinks he has a complaint discovers, when he tries to put it into words to his boss, that it simply does not hold up. If the boss listens sympathetically and is diplomatic in handling the situation, he saves the employee's pride and prevents

his embarrassment. In the adjustment of grievances it is important to make sure a subordinate is never discredited or suffers a loss of face.

3. *Investigate carefully.* Never act on hearsay information or jump to conclusions about an employee's guilt or innocence on the basis of his record. Check the facts—not only those that support your personal views, but those that run counter to them. Give careful consideration to the employee's case as expressed in his grievance before you dismiss any evidence presented in it because it is not in line with information you have previously received. Test its truth by thoroughly investigating it.

4. *Understand the intent of the contract provision.* Do not accept the advice of a shop steward or an employee on the interpretation of a provision in the contract, especially on the way a particular type of dispute has been settled in the past. If you are uncertain as to the meaning of the applicable section of the agreement, ask the advice of your company labor relations people. You are a representative of management, and if you make unauthorized or foolish commitments, it can be very costly.

5. *Be fair.* Consistency and objective firmness is the only sound policy in grievance handling. Resolve each complaint on the basis of what is fair, not who made it. The fastest way to undermine your own authority is to attempt to placate an aggressive union steward or a trouble-making employee by giving special concessions in the settlement of grievances. It is also dangerous to play favorites and allow certain employees (for example, highly skilled and needed workers, or workers who are your particular friends) to take special liberties denied to others. There must be fair, even-handed justice in the administration of company rules or employees will lose faith in the grievance procedure and in your leadership.

6. *Maintain proper records.* Records are the foundation of efficient administration. They provide documentary evidence of past decisions and actions. Occasionally you may need to refer to

them to justify the way you handled a grievance at an arbitration hearing. Adequate records assure consistency. With them you can check past decisions to make sure present ones are in line with precedent and practice. Records also serve as your fact sheet if you are ever asked to justify your actions at a higher step of the grievance procedure or at arbitration.

7. *Keep your superior informed.* Tell him of any important decisions you have made or contemplate making in unusual or touchy grievance situations. He is entitled to full information on activities in his department. It enables him to correct mistakes before too much damage has been done.

8. *Protect management's rights.* The union-management agreement is negotiated personnel policy covering all matters concerning the wages, hours, and working conditions of employees within a particular bargaining unit. The rights that management has obtained under such an agreement have been obtained through the hard process of negotiation, and possibly important concessions have been made to secure them. Understand the importance of management's negotiated rights and enforce them. If they are improperly or inconsistently applied, or not exercised at all, they may be lost.

9. *Get advice in making decisions on broadly written contract provisions.* Such provisions are sometimes referred to as "accordion clauses," and they may be subject to various interpretations. If such a clause is stretched, "anything goes"; if the interpretation is too precise, many grievances are likely. Good judgment is essential in making decisions when the contract provision applicable to the situation is of this kind. Such matters as lunch periods, coffee breaks, leaves of absence, and washup times are the type of items sometimes covered by so-called accordion clauses.

10. *Settle grievances promptly.* Never allow employee complaints to come to a boil by leaving them to simmer on a back burner. Lack of action and dilatoriness in grievance handling only make things worse. Of course it would be foolish to be so intent

on the prompt adjustment of grievances that expedient or unsound settlements are made. Always take the time needed to investigate the facts, but make it a rule to give the employee an answer to his grievance together with the reasons for the answer as quickly as possible.

11. *Never try to conceal mistakes.* Nobody's perfect. When you have erred in handling a grievance, admit it and set matters straight. The biggest blunder a leader can make is trying to hide a wrong decision or action or to bluff his way out of it. Employees do not expect a boss to provide them with error-free leadership, but they do think they are entitled to honesty.

12. *Consider the long-range consequences of your decision.* Do not settle a grievance simply to get it out of the way. Do your best to determine the effect the settlement will have, not only on the aggrieved employee, but on the group and on management-union relations in general. An expedient or "special favor" adjustment of a grievance may solve the immediate problem. But it may also establish a precedent and create far more serious problems for you later.

13. *Avoid sharp practices.* Outsmarting a shop steward or an employee may help you win an argument, but in the long run you are likely to lose far more than your short-term gain. Even though you may be within your rights and justified on technical grounds, a decision that imposes an injustice or an inequity on an employee creates bad feelings and is unfair.

14. *Accept your leadership responsibility.* As management's first-line administrator of the union agreement and the company's policies and rules relating to labor relations, it is up to you to understand the intent of the agreement and to know how the policies and rules it describes are to be applied. To the employees you are the company's representative. This is a key responsibility. Employees judge your performance as a leader by the way you exercise it.

THE WRITTEN REPLY TO THE
FORMAL GRIEVANCE

Many agreements require that all formal grievances receive a reply in writing and thus become a part of the permanent record. When what you say is for the record, it is most important to express yourself accurately and carefully. Furthermore, your ability to give a written answer to an official grievance is an indication of your skill in looking at a problem, analyzing it, and reaching a sound decision on what to do about it.

When you have carefully studied the grievance, reviewed both the union agreement and operating practice to make sure that your decision is consistent with the terms of the former and with precedent, and are certain of the reliability of your information and your ability to prove it, you are fully prepared to write an intelligent reply to an employee's complaint.

Be sure your answer deals with the specific issues of the employee's complaint and does this plainly. Occasionally the responses of supervisors have so carefully sidestepped the issues involved and been so vague that it is difficult to determine what they are trying to say.

A harsh denial of a grievance written in abrupt or unfeeling language may cause unnecessary resentment on the part of the employee, even though the decision itself may be perfectly proper. So try to help the employee understand and (if you reject his complaint) accept your decision. A properly written response may be useful to you and the union as a guide in handling future situations of a similar nature.

Do not hesitate to get advice if you need help in replying to a grievance. It will protect you from mistakes, increase your knowledge of labor relations, and add to your proficiency in carrying out this important responsibility.

The following suggestions may be useful when writing a reply to a formal grievance.

A. Make sure your answer includes:
 1. A brief summary of the case
 2. A short review of the main points at issue
 3. A clearly written statement explaining the reasons behind your decision on each issue raised and a short concluding statement which provides your reply to the grievance as a whole

B. Make sure you know:
 1. What facts relate directly to the dispute and which ones are irrelevant
 2. The past employment record of the grievant. (This is particularly important if the grievance concerns the alleged imposition of an excessive penalty.)
 3. What provisions of the agreement relate to the issue. (If such provisions are broad or vague or if the contract is silent on the subject, check past practice.)

C. Make certain you reply to such questions as:
 1. Who? (Employee's name and job classification)
 2. What? (All pro and con information regarding the dispute)
 3. Where? (Location of occurrence)
 4. When? (Date, month, and time of day event took place)
 5. How? (Check facts for accuracy.)

D. Make sure you can answer these questions:
 1. Are your facts sustained by company records?
 2. Will reliable witnesses testify to their accuracy?
 3. Are you positive there are no gaps in your case, and that you are not taking anything for granted?

DANGER SPOTS IN GRIEVANCE HANDLING

If you read the *National Labor Relations Reporter's* accounts of arbitration cases and decisions resulting from them, you will see that most of the rulings that have gone against management have been based on mistakes that managers have made in administering the grievance procedure. Unions have had great success in winning the support of arbitrators when they have shown that supervisors have made technical errors in procedure, have ignored precedent or been inconsistent in applying it, have imposed excessive penalties for offenses, or have committed some act that has seemed arbitrary, discriminatory, or in violation of the union agreement. True, most of the supervisors' mistakes may have been unintentional, but because of them guilty employees have escaped punishment or had it substantially reduced. All this the experienced supervisor understands, for he has learned, probably the hard way, the danger spots in grievance handling and is careful to avoid them. You can, too, if you keep in mind that when management loses its arguments at arbitration, some supervisor probably made one of the following blunders:

1. *Failed to plan properly.* It takes sound planning to handle a grievance properly. All too often supervisors, pushed by other work, fail to take the time necessary and attempt to improvise decisions, trusting in general knowledge, good luck, and instinct to pull them through. Unfortunately, this approach is likely to be unsuccessful. Care and attention must be given to details. If they are overlooked, they may become stumbling blocks later on.

2. *Had only a sketchy knowledge of the union agreement.* You can usually be absolutely certain that the shop steward knows what the agreement says. Furthermore, he knows how to use the agreement to his advantage if you let him. That is his job. So do not take chances! If you do not know or are not quite sure exactly what is contained in a provision of your agreement or how it should be interpreted, do not base your decision on a good guess. Make certain you are right, even if this means discussing the matter with staff experts. The shop steward wins many of his cases because of supervisory mistakes and procedural errors.

3. *Investigated carelessly.* Do not rely on hearsay evidence. It is

always the wise course to see for yourself. Hasty decisions based on the unsubstantiated story of an assistant or some employee have caused many a supervisory ruling to be reversed, with consequent loss of face for both the supervisor and the company.

4. *Did not read facts accurately.* Facts are of little value if they are misinterpreted. Study all information carefully and make sure you are interpreting it properly before you decide what to do.

5. *Put off making a decision.* Putting off a grievance decision until tomorrow only makes things more difficult. The employee wants a "Yes" or "No" answer to his complaint. The sooner you give it to him, the better it will be for employee relations in general.

6. *Refused to recognize changed circumstances.* No book will provide an automatic solution to every problem. Sometimes precedent is not a guide, and the agreement itself, instead of giving precise directions, probably leaves plenty of room for you to exercise your judgment. Conditions change and an organization must adjust to changing circumstances. Precedent is important, but only if it is pertinent to the case you are considering.

7. *Refused to make exceptions to the rules.* Consistency in the administration of discipline and employee relations generally is highly desirable, but mental rigidity is not. Good rules should usually be observed. But it is unwise management to make a decision that works a hardship on an employee or that is unfair to him for the sake of a rule or simply to uphold consistency. If, because of unusual circumstances surrounding a case, the imposition of a penalty in a particular situation is unjust, or if upholding a rule deprives an employee of an opportunity that he should rightfully have, you should consider making an exception. Talk the problem over with your superior and your labor experts. Solutions to such problems can likely be found without establishing unwise precedents.

8. *Failed to anticipate future problems.* The experienced super-

visor prevents many grievances from occurring by identifying up-coming problems that may annoy or worry employees: for ex-ample, changes in job content, changes in methods or techniques, and the introduction of new machines. Abrupt changes made without notice are an almost sure way to cause complaints, and a good supervisor does his best to alleviate fear and worry about job security by explaining the reasons for such changes and how they will affect employees well in advance of making them.

9. *Failed to follow the course of grievances.* The mere fact that a supervisor is unable to settle a grievance at his level is no excuse for forgetting about it. He still shares in the responsibility for its final solution. If there are needless delays by higher management in the determination of the dispute, encourage your superiors to speed up the process. The employee wants an answer. Slowness can cause you difficulties.

10. *Magnified the weaknesses of the grievance procedure.* The grievance machinery has built-in faults usually attributed to the people responsible for operating it. Nevertheless, it is a tested and proven system of industrial justice that safeguards the employee's rights, gives him a means of bringing his complaints to the atten-tion of management, and, if administered properly, protects the rights of management. True, it takes time and trouble to settle grievances. But it is important to do so. The effort spent today in the sensible adjustment of employee complaints pays off tomorrow in positive human relations.

A SUPERVISOR'S GUIDELINES FOR DEALING WITH A UNION STEWARD

The union is the representative af all employees in all matters re-lating to wages, hours, and working conditions, and usually the shop steward is its spokesman. As such he is the advocate of the members of the union at grievance hearings, assists them in the preparation of their arguments, and presents these at the hearing. His is an elected office, and his tenure depends on how well employees believe he is serving them, so he wants to do it aggressively and well. The probability is he has received some training for his duties—the majority of unions provide such training—and you can generally be sure he has been given special instruction in grievance handling. The union agreement is his law book, and he fully understands the importance of precedent in the settlement of disputes. He also is likely to know procedure backward and forward and is quick to take full advantage of technical errors made by supervisors whenever doing so will further the interest of a client. In the grievance procedure he has the initiative and is on the offensive. The very submission of a grievance requires management to justify its decisions or actions.

These rules may be useful to you in working constructively with the union shop steward:

1. *Understand the function of the union steward.* The steward holds an official and responsible position. He is spokesman for the employees. He will do his best to get favorable rulings on their grievances. That is his job. This does not make him your enemy. Nor is he simply a trouble-making nuisance when he pushes a case for an employee that you know and he knows has little substance. It is not his responsibility to tell a client to forget about his complaint because it has no merit. That is your job, and it is also your job to explain why in reasonable, clear, and persuasive language. Nor is it part of a shop steward's duties to make your work easier. So control your anger if he makes highly exaggerated claims or statements that have no basis in facts, or if he attacks you personally. He may be trying to make you lose your temper, your head, and your case. He has a political office and wants to earn a reputation as a man who stands up to management and who gets things done for employees.

2. *Do not accept "blue-sky" complaints as formal grievances.*

Listen to all employee complaints and gripes and do your best to resolve them if you can. But do not admit a grievance to the formal grievance procedure unless it meets the contract definition as to what will be accepted as a formal grievance.

3. *Keep to the facts.* Do not let a shop steward trap you into becoming involved in angry arguments or emotional issues that have no bearing on the case. They are probably red herrings anyway, intended to bolster his weak arguments. Your responsibility is to administer your company's agreement and to avoid special or favorable rulings that are inconsistent with practice. It takes a cool head and calm judgment to do this.

4. *Build a relationship of mutual respect between you and the shop steward.* This is done by making firm, fair, and consistent decisions. You cannot make the steward your partner. Nor will you win him over by doing him favors. However, if you win the steward's respect for your integrity and his trust in your fairness, you have created the kind of relationship that makes the adjustment of grievances easier. You earn respect by giving it. The shop steward and other officials of the union have their jobs to perform. You cannot find fault with them so long as they do their work in a legitimate manner and exercise the rights that are allowed them under the agreement. True, they are usually on the opposite side of the issue that comes up in labor relations. It is also true that the shop steward may be a hard antagonist at a grievance hearing. But if you are a professional, you recognize that the two of you have many mutual interests, and that the most important of them is to keep the organization functioning successfully.

5. *Never make unofficial or off-the-record agreements with the union.* Keep all of your dealings on top of the table. Secret understandings and "gentlemen's agreements" with the shop steward may serve the interest of expediency, but they are likely to lead to severe trouble. Never make promises you may not be able to deliver, and remember that the shop steward may not be able to ful-

fill any secret commitment he has made to you. Furthermore, he may not even be reelected, and his successor has no obligation to honor past off-the-record agreements.

6. *Keep your poise when confronted by manufactured grievances.* There are times when a union intentionally stirs up trouble and as part of its strategy floods management with contrived grievances. You know the difference between a real grievance and a political one. So if you suddenly begin to get a number of the latter, you will know that the union is planning a move and that higher management should be informed about it as quickly as possible. It is top management's responsibility to develop a consistent plan of action to counter this kind of situation.

EIGHT

How to Step Up Efficiency
through Better Performance Appraisal

Every manager "rates" or appraises the abilities, intelligence, skills, and dependability of the people who work for him. He may not do so formally or systematically; indeed, his method may be random and impressionistic. But nevertheless, he knows, or thinks he knows, which subordinates work efficiently and well, which ones he can depend on in emergencies, and which ones will accept hard, demanding tasks and carry them out successfully. He gains this knowledge through observation and experience, and on it he bases such decisions as who will be given what assignments, who will receive merit increases, promotions, or transfers, and, conversely, who will be downgraded or terminated because of poor performance or improper attitudes.

The purpose of a formal method of appraisal is to put objectivity into performance rating and to free it as much as possible from such human shortcomings as prejudice, favoritism, and guesswork.

A systematic approach is intended to assure the employee that his boss will review his total performance and not judge his work impressionistically or on the basis of a few assignments which he happens to remember. It also protects a subordinate from being ignored or overlooked and perhaps not receiving the recognition for his performance that it rightfully deserves.

Today nearly all companies of any size have adopted some method of formal appraisal. Methods range from a simple ranking plan to the more complex and, from the point of view of the supervisor, certainly more time-consuming plan of appraisal by objectives. But all systems are founded on certain fundamental assumptions, among which are:

1. Supervisors should know their employees individually, and the very act of rating subordinates and advising them how to improve their performances is one way to promote a better superior-subordinate relationship.

2. All employees want to know and need to know how they are doing on their jobs, what parts of them they are performing satisfactorily, and where and how they should improve, and appraisal interviews provide them with this information.

Briefly, then, the main purpose of an appraisal program is to improve employee performance. Industry has learned from experience that employees who have the benefit of systematic and periodic appraisal interviews with their supervisors have better attitudes toward their jobs and their companies.

THE BENEFITS OF PERFORMANCE APPRAISAL

The policy manual of most major American corporations usually contains a statement on performance appraisal that is generally prefaced with a few sentences reading something like this:

> Our most important and valuable asset is our employees. Among the major responsibilities of our executives and supervisors at all levels of our company is to train, develop, and advise their sub-

ordinates with the objective to help them maximize their skills and talents and to treat them in a fair and just manner. We expect our supervisors to know their employees as individuals, and for this reason we have established a plan of performance appraisal which is used uniformly by all of our managers. The purpose of the plan is to encourage and assist the individual employee in his growth and development by evaluating all aspects of his job performance, and then to provide him with specific help and counsel in order to help him help himself to improve. The intelligent and consistent administration of this plan will produce additional results which will benefit the organization as a whole.

The results listed will be something like this:

1. The plan will become a guide to the supervisor in planning and implementing the training of employees.

2. It will eliminate appraisals based on inadequate knowledge or guesswork and assure the employee that every aspect of his performance will be evaluated when he is appraised.

3. It will improve employee attitudes and raise morale because it demonstrates to each employee that his supervisor is personally interested in his development and sincerely desirous of helping him achieve his full potential.

4. It will provide the company with information it needs in deciding promotions and transfers and will help management properly utilize the talents of its personnel.

5. It will be useful in identifying and making records of special talents, skills, and capabilities of employees not presently being used.

6. It will be helpful in determining which employees deserve merit increases for outstanding performance.

7. It will give the employee an opportunity to discuss privately both his job and his future problems with his supervisor, and in such discussions the employee will learn exactly how well he is doing and in what areas of his work he needs to improve.

8. It will require supervisors to do more than point out an employee's shortcomings by stipulating that each supervisor, when

criticizing an employee's deficiency, be prepared to offer advice, counsel, and, when needed, remedial training to help the employee improve.

It would be foolish to claim that any system which must rely on fallible human judgment can ever become error free. But a good appraisal system is far more likely to convince workers that they are being judged fairly than is the lack of one, which permits the supervisor to evaluate employees on his personal opinions alone and leaves them completely in the dark as to what factors relating to their work are most important in getting a good rating. Also, it precludes negative remarks from supervisors, such as, "Don't worry about how you are doing. When you are not doing all right, I'll be the first to tell you."

The majority of personnel authorities say that negative results arising from appraisal interviews seldom are long-lasting, and even if an employee's initial reaction to criticism from his boss is resentment, he will soon have second thoughts and conclude that some of his superior's comments were very true indeed. In this case he will probably decide that in his own interests he should try to eliminate faults, and thus a desirable change in his behavioral pattern will have been accomplished.

Attitude studies have shown that employee reaction to formal appraisal reviews is generally favorable. Comments frequently quoted in such reports include:

> "It gives you a chance to talk to your boss about your job and to bring out problems that are bothering you that you don't get a chance to discuss in daily contacts."

> "They (the counseling interviews) have been helpful to me. I had the opportunity to give my opinions, and at least I know how the boss thinks I'm doing."

> "I didn't agree with all of his comments. But mostly what he said was correct, and it's encouraging to know that he wants to help me improve."

THE LIMITATIONS OF
PERFORMANCE APPRAISAL

Policies are hopeful statements of intentions and frequently have become considerably different in practice from what the policy framers had originally expected.

Formal appraisal systems or merit ratings are viewed cynically by some operating managers as "so much more paperwork cooked up for us by the personnel department." And they may think the result of a particular rating is not necessarily a true reflection of the rated employee's actual performance. How often have you heard such comments as, "Why don't they make it easy and ask if I am satisfied with the way So-and-So is doing his job?" or, "How am I going to answer all of the questions? Some of them don't even apply to my people," or, "Why do they keep on changing the questions? Don't they think I'm giving the right answers?" Furthermore, if over the years you have rated the same employee five or six times, you may allow the process to become routine, believing that you already know all there is to know about what he can or cannot do, and that therefore there is no reason to take up too much time with the interview.

However, if you know the limitations of appraisal systems and some of the human faults that cause them to fail to accomplish their objectives as completely as management might wish, you can at least guard against the faults in your own practices. Here are some of them.

1. *Appraisals sometimes cause supervisory resentment.* A typical appraisal form contains a long list of factors on which the employee is to be rated. A supervisor may regard the task of completing such a rating as a time-wasting and tedious undertaking. He may also consider the form itself an indication that his management does not believe he knows how to judge the individual performance of various subordinates, and this may make him re-

sentful. Finally, he may be critical of certain details in the form, such as "forced choice," or he may think that the number of gradations on the form describing the quality of the employee's work does not permit him sufficient flexibility to give accurate answers. If he has this attitude, he may consider his part in the appraisal system as a test of wits with the personnel department and try to outsmart the experts instead of rating the employee.

2. *The supervisor may not be too familiar with the work of all of the employees he is supposed to appraise.* There are often comparatively new workers in a group, and it may be impossible for a supervisor to give them more than an impressionistic appraisal. Furthermore, it is sometimes true that a supervisor does not have sufficient information to answer all of the questions even if a veteran employee is involved; in fact, even his interpretation of some of the questions may vary from their intent. For these reasons he may not have too much faith in the final scores of the appraisals and may even think the weighting of the different factors is out of line and unrealistic.

3. *Some supervisors tend to seek a middle ground.* They may seek to protect themselves from higher-management criticism of their ratings by avoiding extremes. They may think it safe to score nearly all employees "average" instead of marking some "outstanding" or "below standard." This rating habit is described by personnel people as the "centrist tendency"; it shows that the supervisor either lacks sufficient knowledge to make precise appraisals or, in the case of unsatisfactory employees, is inclined to generosity and gives them higher evaluations than they deserve.

4. *Some supervisors give high ratings to employees on the basis of one or two qualities.* This trait, known to experts as the "halo effect," defeats the entire purpose of employee performance appraisal. If a supervisor permits himself to be blinded by a particular attribute of an employee (for example, an articulate person's gift with words which covers up his lack of ability in many parts of his work), that employee may get high ratings on such factors

as "initiative" and "dependability" even though his actual performance does not merit such praise.

5. *Some supervisors give poor ratings to employees on the basis of one or two qualities.* These supervisors suffer from what is called the "pitchfork tendency," the reverse of the halo effect. A quality or fault of an employee which they do not like causes them to be hypercritical of his overall performance, and they rate him accordingly.

6. *The standards of various supervisors differ, and this affects consistency of ratings in general.* Some supervisors err on the generous side and are inclined to rate nearly all of their employees on the high side. Others take the opposite path and are too critical. An employee who comes up with a rating that is a little above average in the department of a supervisor of the latter type might have enjoyed appraisals as "superior" when he worked in another department. When you consider the tendency of a few supervisors to rate overcritically or overgenerously, and when you remember that the average supervisor probably is holding fast to the center ground and scoring the majority of his people in the middle range of ratings, you are not surprised that certain operating managers are inclined to question the value of ratings as a whole and to put little faith in them.

The defects of formal performance appraisal systems lie not so much with the systems but with the people who are supposed to make them work. For even the counseling interview that is supposed to help the employee improve his performance may be damaging if it is not done properly. Constructive criticism of an employee's job performance may undermine his self-confidence and give him a feeling of insecurity. Experts in the personnel field also caution that praise is not likely to have much effect one way or the other on the ability of an employee to attain his particular job objectives, although certainly there are few people who do not enjoy receiving it. And there is no escaping the fact that some supervisors are simply poor counselors. Their ratings may be extremely accurate, but somehow they are unable to transmit helpful advice or constructive criticism to employees in a way that provides them with the incentive to work harder to develop their skills and talents.

In addition all employees do not respond well to a critical appraisal interview, and there are certain things you can seldom hope to accomplish with all subordinates no matter how able and conscientious you may be in interviewing and counseling.

To be realistic:

▪ If you are honest in your comments, there is no approach open to you that will make a highly critical appraisal interview a happy occasion for either you or the employee.

▪ It is unlikely that the best counseling and advice will transform an innately suspicious and distrustful employee into a trustful and self-assured one.

▪ Counseling does not often make a hostile, belligerent employee cooperative and pleasant—at least, not overnight.

▪ You can seldom persuade a defensive and insecure employee to become self-critical and confident by advising him to do so.

▪ You cannot help an employee who simply lacks the talent, skill, knowledge, or temperament to do a particular job to become skilled at performing it.*

HOW TO MAKE CRITICISM LESS DIFFICULT

Despite the obvious benefits gained from the effective evaluation and counseling of employees, many supervisors have a distaste for doing it, especially when it involves criticism. To be on the receiving end of criticism is never pleasant, but it is also difficult to sit down and in a calm, detached manner remark on the shortcomings of another.

* Robert Hoppock, cited in J. M. Black, *Personnel Management*, Lincoln Management Development Service, Cleveland, Ohio, 1971.

Yale Laitin, a management consultant, once said, "We don't like to judge another person's weaknesses and describe them to him because most of us don't like to be criticized for our own weaknesses." And Schuyler D. Hoslett, of the Reuben H. Donnelly Corporation, observed, "Many of the problems in industrial organizations arise not because people are not nice enough, but because people, especially superiors working with subordinates, will not always face up to difficult problems in human relations."

Although it may be hard to criticize a subordinate, still it must be done if he is to improve. A basic management responsibility is to report the bad news as well as the good, and a boss does his subordinate no favor by attempting to spare his feelings. The average employee is usually well aware of his shortcomings if he is not doing his job (or any part of it) satisfactorily, and if his boss appears to be satisfied with below-standard performance, the employee assumes the boss simply does not care. The employee becomes frustrated and indifferent, and his performance may become even worse.

The best way to avoid having to make major criticisms of an employee's work during a formal appraisal interview is to have frequent, even daily, contacts with him and discuss his difficulties and job-related problems. The closer your relationship with subordinates and the more accessible you are, the easier it becomes for you to praise or criticize. Your comments occur immediately after or even during the events that cause them. The facts are fresh, and the employee realizes exactly what you are talking about. Praise becomes more meaningful, and criticism, particularly if you are showing the employee how to correct a faulty job practice or perform his assignment more efficiently is more helpful and easier to take. Finally, a person is generally more willing to accept adverse comments about his performance, or even his attitude or personal habits, from someone he likes and respects than he is from a stranger.

THE ADVANTAGES OF ACCESSIBILITY

The supervisor who is remote from his subordinates is rarely effective as a counselor. His aloofness denies him an intimate knowledge of his people's work, and he probably must rely on records, his general impressions, or the comments of an assistant for the information he does have. Therefore he tends to be vague in his criticisms, and he may also be inclined to undercriticize or overpraise because by doing so he avoids controversy. An employee leaving an interview with such a supervisor may have no real understanding of what his boss actually thinks of his performance; or he may not even know whether he is carrying out his responsibilities properly.

Daily talks with employees on the job are natural and part of on-the-job training, so you are simply performing your supervisory duties when you introduce comments about the specifics of an employee's work into such discussions. The employee expects you to do no less and is generally glad to have the chance to explain his job problems or difficulties and get your advice on what to do about them. What you say in such a situation—whether you praise or criticize—seems natural and in proportion. If you wait three months until the next appraisal period to mention a fault, the employee may have forgotten all about the incident and be resentful that you dredged it up. Moreover, by such a delay you lose the spontaneity and lack of tension characteristic of the informal talk. Everything seems cold and artificial.

There are many other advantages to maintaining a close supervisory relationship with subordinates. Here are some of them.

1. If you instruct on a daily basis, and praise and criticize the same way, the employee always knows how he is doing.

2. The formal appraisal interview can become a friendly discussion review at which the employee feels free to talk openly about his interests, problems, and ambitions.

3. You gain insight into the employee as a person, enabling you to do a better job of supervising him.

4. Frequent and informal appraisal discussions help the employee identify his shortcomings or faults and correct them. The sequel to the appraisal interview is training. Any veteran instructor knows that you cannot "teach it all at one session." Good instruction is done on a step-by-step basis.

5. Daily contacts with employees give the supervisor an opportunity to note employee progress and to offer encouragement.

6. A supervisor's accessibility and willingness to listen to employees' problems and to encourage their suggestions are important factors in the creation of a good working climate. All relations between him and his subordinates become more relaxed and easier.

THE BASIC APPROACHES TO
APPRAISAL INTERVIEWING

There are essentially three methods that a supervisor uses in the conduct of an appraisal interview. Two are traditional and are usually described as the "Tell and Sell" and the "Tell and Listen" plans. The third, a more subjective approach, is basically a problem-solving technique. Management by objectives and its variants are increasingly popular plans of appraisal that fall into this category.

The "Tell and Sell" and "Tell and Listen" approaches are applied precisely as their names indicate. Neither is as demanding as are the completely consultative requirements of problem solving, nor do they require as much supervisory time. In "Tell and Sell," the boss merely explains to the subordinate what parts of his assignment he is performing well and in what areas he could improve, and then tries to convince him that he should change his job habits accordingly. "Tell and Listen" requires the supervisor to identify the employee's strong points and deficiencies and, in the second part of the interview, to encourage him to describe his reaction to the discussion and the evaluation. The latter method is more demanding, as it asks the boss to explore the employee's attitudes and feelings, and this means his approach must incorporate many of the indirect techniques used in problem solving. However, both methods put the superior in the position of being judge and make his decisions final.

Problem solving, however, is almost entirely nondirective. The supervisor seeks not only to investigate the employee's attitudes and motivations, but to stimulate his development by persuading him to discuss the problems, ideas, satisfactions, and disappointments he has encountered since the last time he was evaluated. He is also encouraged to share in setting his own performance goals. Such a system is usually described as "Management by Objectives (MBO)," and some companies claim remarkable results. It is necessary to acquire great interviewing expertness to make it work.

If MBO works successfully, it shifts the emphasis of employee appraisal from the supervisor to employee self-analysis and also turns the ratee's attention away from the past to the future. In this way it helps him relate his career planning to the actual needs and realities of his company. An MBO plan calls for the supervisor to work with the employee as a consultant, on the theory that their discussions regarding the employee's job problems and goals will improve and strengthen their relationship. The chief concern of the supervisor is to determine what he can do to help the employee reach his objectives.

The advantages of MBO might be listed as follows:

1. It helps employees establish realistic and challenging objectives.

2. It (like other appraisal plans) supplies a method of detecting training requirements.

3. It encompasses the entire process of developing an employee's

ability to identify a problem, decide how to solve it, and by his own action turn his ideas into accomplishment.

4. It gives the employee a greater sense of achievement and satisfaction because it enables him to measure his progress against his own objectives instead of against his superior's.

5. It gives both the supervisor and the employee greater flexibility in the establishment of objectives and doing what is necessary to achieve them.

However, MBO does not always find a happy home in the company that installs it. There are dangers that must be taken into account and guarded against.

1. MBO does not eliminate the quirks of character or personal peculiarities of a particular boss in his relationship with employees.

2. Sometimes the improved relationship between boss and employee that is supposed to come about simply does not occur; in fact, some experts think that any hostility or resentment that there may have been between the two prior to MBO is actually increased by the plan because it does not consider all of the many and complex aspects of motivation.

3. Facts and figures on an employee's performance are concentrated on short-term objectives. This means an employee may devote so much of his time to achieving his goals that he lets other parts of his work go by the board.*

There are other defects in MBO that behavioral scientists have noted, but still the stress the plan places on an employee's participation in the appraisal process and in formulating and developing a program to attain his own goals has won many supporters.

The particular method of performance appraisal that you use depends either on the plan your company has installed or the method that you have developed through your own experience and that best fits your personality and supervisory style. Furthermore,

* H. J. Chruden and A. W. Sherman, *Personnel Management*, Southwestern Publishing Co., Cincinnati, Ohio, 1972.

the purpose of this chapter is not to provide an in-depth study of appraisal methods, but to give you certain principles of performance evaluation and of the conduct of an effective appraisal interview that are applicable in nearly all situations, regardless of the method. Together with these principles are given certain suggestions that personnel authorities have found will make you more effective in your discussions with employees regarding the quality of their work.

THE APPRAISAL INTERVIEW

It is a serious mistake to attempt to improvise an appraisal interview, simply relying on your general knowledge of an employee's performance. You need facts, and records are essential in supplying facts. You should review these records prior to the discussion. They include the employee's production, attendance, and disciplinary records. It is important also to check the quantity and quality of his production. Information of this kind gives specificity to your comments and thus helps you avoid general or vague criticisms that may not even be accurate and that are quite likely to provoke the employee's resentment.

It is also advisable to study the employee's job description before the interview in order to refresh your memory as to the exact nature of his responsibilities and duties. This review enables you to compare the various requirements of his job with the competence he has demonstrated in carrying out each one of them.

Your preparation should also cover the planning of the structure of the interview itself. If you have a clear idea of what he has done and where he needs to improve, you know what to criticize, what to commend. Furthermore, you can prepare a tentative plan of corrective training or self-help, and this will make your counseling more effective.

In general, the interview should be divided into five parts: (1) the introduction or warm-up; (2) a review of the employee's overall performance; (3) your comments on the employee's strengths and deficiencies; (4) the employee's expression of his reaction to your criticism; (5) the program recommended for his improvement and your mutual sugestions for its implementation. The purpose of the introduction is to create a relaxed atmosphere in which an effective interview can be conducted. Fear and tension raise barriers in communications, and both are frequently present in an appraisal interview. The very idea of appraisal is most upsetting to some employees. Not many people enjoy going to a meeting the only purpose of which is to analyze their past performances and perhaps hold them up to criticism. Employees usually want to know where they stand with their boss, but most of them like to have the ordeal of "being told" over with. So you can understand why there is usually some degree of employee apprehension regarding the evaluation interview. It has already been noted that the best way to reduce this is by daily contacts with employees. Then the formal appraisal interview is no longer terrifying and they can take part in the discussion in a more positive frame of mind.

A few friendly questions or comments are usually sufficient to establish the proper interviewing cnvironment and relax the subordinate. When you think this has been accomplished, your next move is to describe, if necessary, how the evaluation system functions and to explain the standards against which you are comparing the employee's performance. You should also tell him the factors on which he is being judged and their order of importance. Here you are provided with the opportunity to comment on the advantages he derives from a good appraisal system which enables you and him cooperatively to identify his training needs and to develop programs to meet them.

It is frequently possible to form an accurate judgment of how a subordinate will respond to any adverse remarks you may make later by the way he responds to your explanation of the appraisal system and the job standards. For example, if he thinks the system itself is unfair and considers the job standards unreasonable, it is almost certain that he will be defensive about his own record and quick to argue with you about any part of it that you tell him is unsatisfactory.

There are two ways of covering an employee's general performance in an appraisal interview. You can summarize, explaining broadly what, in your opinion, are his strong points and his deficiencies. Or you can ask him to tell you frankly how he would rate himself.

In all likelihood, the average employee's self-evaluation of his performance will not be too different from your own. Most people know what they are doing well and where they could stand improvement. If anything, an employee is likely to be more critical of his performance than you would be. This may be due partly to modesty. But most people are aware of their faults, and if they face the choice of having to admit them or having their boss expose them, they prefer the former.

Commenting on an employee's deficiency constructively requires tact and considerable skill. When you make such criticisms, be certain to back them up with examples. It has already been emphasized that generalities in performance appraisal produce a negative effect, but the point is so important it should be emphasized by a remark of the late Elliott Janney, noted management consultant, who said, "You can destroy a subordinate's confidence with a critical generality. If you want him to improve, be precise. He may not agree with you, but at least he'll know what you are talking about."

There are certain employees who simply cannot take criticism even if it is intended for their own good. They exist in sort of a "no news is good news" vacuum and think it far better to hear no criticism at all than it is to receive helpful criticism, including good advice as to what they can do to correct the faults which are holding them back. But even if an employee reacts poorly to evaluation, the process is still of value to you. It has revealed his emotional immaturity and shows that he is not a good risk for more important duties.

It is never easy to criticize deliberately another's shortcomings however well intentioned your criticism may be. But, then, many aspects of the leadership responsibility impose a heavy burden. Certainly a supervisor would be neglecting his duty to his subordinate if he dodged his obligation to tell that subordinate where and how he was deficient, or if he was so kindly and gentle in his comments that the employee did not understand what he was talking about. If you want to help a person improve, there is no escaping the job evaluation interview.

A GUIDE AND A CHECKLIST TO MORE EFFICIENT APPRAISAL INTERVIEWING

Dr. Robert Hoppock of New York University, a well-known writer in the personnel field, has compiled suggestions to improve one's effectiveness in appraisal interviewing. Here is a summary of them.

1. Before you discuss the man, discuss the job. You and your subordinate may have different ideas about the exact nature of his responsibilities. In doing this a job description is helpful. Preview it together to see if it needs revision.

2. Ask before you tell. Ask the employee what he thinks are his strengths, his weaknesses. He can criticize himself more readily than he can accept criticism.

3. Listen. The effectiveness of the interview will increase with your understanding of the man you are counseling. If you talk when he wants to talk, you may miss some of the best opportunities you ever had to find out what makes him tick.

4. If the subordinate appraises himself more favorably than you do, invite him to tell you why. Then if you still disagree, restate his self-appraisal. Let him see that you want him to consider his judgment as well as your own, and that his feelings are important even if you disagree. Then explain why you disagree.

5. In appraising a man's mistakes, consider the number of his mistakes in proportion to the number of decisions he has had to make; consider how much freedom he was given to act on his own judgment; try to recall his performance over a long period of time. In comparing mistakes of two men, consider the relative difficulties of the tasks assigned to them.

6. Try not to be unduly influenced by things that affect your feelings but do not otherwise affect a man's value to the company. (If he has a practice that differs from yours but still gets results, do not let your dislike of the practice affect your judgment.)

7. When you must criticize, criticize the man's performance, not the man himself. He may be able to improve his performance but he may not be able to change his personality.

8. If you are partly at fault, admit it.

9. If you want cooperation, do not undertake a performance review too soon after you have had to reprimand an employee.

10. Never discuss another person's performance with the man you are appraising.

11. Do not discuss salary raises or promotions during an appraisal interview.

12. In an appraisal interview, it is not necessary for you and the subordinate to agree on everything.

13. Be yourself. Do not try to copy someone else's methods if they do not fit your personality.

14. If the employee is really deficient and must be corrected, here are specific things you can do: (a) Let him know exactly where he stands. Otherwise he may think your appraisal is worse than it actually is. (b) If he shows any desire to improve, offer him your help.*

There are other suggestions on interviewing which authorities agree serve to make the process more efficient and rewarding to

* Robert Hoppock, cited in J. M. Black, *Personnel Management*, Lincoln Management Development Service, Cleveland, Ohio, 1971.

both the supervisor and the employee. The following checklist may be useful as a guide to bettering your performance in the appraisal interview and the counseling session that is part of it.

1. *Review your own supervisory practices.* The appraisal interview tells a perceptive supervisor much about his own leadership methods and holds a mirror to his management practices. It provides an opportunity for self-analysis and self-criticism. If an employee has failed to meet your standards of performance, or if his attitude is a detriment to group effectiveness, he certainly merits criticism. But before it is given, review such questions as, "Did I train him properly?" "Were my communications good, my instructions clear?" "Did my own prejudice against the employee play any part in shaping his attitude?" "Did I properly explain to him the responsibilities of his job, and the standards I expected him to meet?" "Did I place him poorly and put him in work that is beyond his ability?" "Did I set him a good example?" "Do I require too much?" Frank answers to such questions will help you face up to your own mistakes or personal faults that may be reflected in the performance of a subordinate. If you accept responsibility for your mistakes, subordinates are more likely to do the same. The ability to examine your performance critically is also insurance that the advice and counseling contained in your criticism of the work of an employee will be detached, objective, and fair.

2. *Make sure you have explained the performance standards the employee is required to meet.* These standards should be fair and within the ability of the employee (if properly trained) to attain. If an employee is not measuring up, tell him exactly how he is not and what he can do to overcome his shortcoming.

3. *Make sure the employee understands the duties of his job.* Certainly, he has a job description which lists his responsibilities, but he may not have read it. Or if he has, he may not have the same understanding that you do regarding the order of priorities.

When you are explaining his duties and their order of importance, give him every opportunity to present his ideas and opinions. It may become abundantly clear that he has different views from yours.

4. *Give comments at the time they are deserved.* Correct an employee's mistakes or criticize his performance or attitude when the situation requires. The same goes for praise. It is most appreciated at the time it is merited. Never save up criticisms and deliver them all at formal appraisal sessions. If you do, you will not accomplish your purpose and you will build unnecessary barriers between you and your employees.

5. *Recognize progress.* When an employee overcomes a fault or shows progress in correcting a shortcoming, a word of encouragement and appreciation is in order. It gives the employee greater incentive to continue to improve.

6. *Do not allow an appraisal session to become a debate.* An objective pro-and-con discussion with an employee regarding his performance is one thing. You want to give him every opportunity to present his side. But a debate or argument over particular points is to be avoided. Give the employee an explanation of the reasons for your evaluations, and do not deny him the opportunity to ask questions about them. But in doing so he should not be permitted to turn the conversation into a controversy. You are responsible for the final evaluation, so there is no need to argue.

7. *Recognize the talents and abilities of the employee.* Employees' talents and abilities are strengths and should be developed. It is the wiser course to help an employee develop his assets and increase his abilities in those parts of his assignment where he has displayed real skill rather than to nag about his weaknesses. An employee should be aware of his shortcomings and strive to minimize them, and perhaps in some cases you could compensate for them by rearranging some of his duties. But to hammer away at a subordinate's faults while you forget about his attributes

gives the appraisal interview a negative emphasis that makes it a dreaded ordeal.

8. *Never package criticism in humor.* True words are often spoken in jest, and with that there is no disputing. But appraisal is a serious business. It concerns the employee's future development. To soft-sell adverse comments by wrapping them in humor, irony, or sarcasm undermines the employee's self-confidence, and he probably resents being the butt of your humor anyway, especially since he has no defense. He may be so angered by the thrust of your language that he remembers only that you were uncomplimentary about his work and he forgets the deficiencies you wanted to bring to his attention. An employee's talents, intelligence, and skill are serious business so far as he is concerned. He wants you to take them and him seriously, for his future may be helped or hindered by your opinions.

9. *Be careful in your use of the so-called "sandwich technique."* The "sandwich technique" is a method of appraisal in which the supervisor first praises the attributes of the employee (to get the interview started right), then criticizes his shortcomings, and finally concludes with praise in order to allow the employee to leave the interview on a high note. The mature employee quickly sees through this approach, which actually signals to him what is coming next. Compliments do not mean much because the employee is bracing himself for the coming criticism. Furthermore, he may be so relieved by your laudatory remarks at the end that he forgets what went before them and believes that any criticism he received is far outweighed by his supervisor's general approval.

10. *Do not search for an appraisal interviewing method that is suitable to every situation.* There is no such thing! The technique you use should be based on interviewing principles that are sound but adjusted to the needs, motivations, and attitudes of the particular subordinate at the other end of the discussion. If you can convince him that you have a sincere interest in his progress and

are anxious to help him develop his talents and abilities, he will probably benefit from the interview and act on your criticisms and advice.

11. *Study the pattern of an employee's performance.* The best way to evaluate an employee's work is to observe it frequently. Discover how he performs under pressure, on housekeeping or routine assignments, on different jobs. Then you can take corrective measures which head off trouble and save you the necessity of criticizing him at a formal interview.

12. *Do not criticize an employee for defects which he cannot do anything about.* If he lacks the skill, intelligence, or talent to do a particular job no matter how hard he tries, criticism will not help. He is a victim of bad placement. Your only choice is to transfer him to less difficult work or to tell him in as kindly a manner as possible that he should try to find a more suitable job elsewhere. He probably realizes his predicament as keenly as you do, and it may even be a relief to him to leave a position which he has no way of filling satisfactorily. In such a situation understanding and sympathy will help him a great deal. He has already lost confidence in himself, and the further humiliation of criticism will do more harm than good.

13. *Be ready with a plan for improvement.* When the evaluation part of the appraisal interview is completed, the counseling session begins. You and the employee have usually agreed on what improvements the latter should make in his work. The question that must be answered next is, "How to do it?" You should have specific advice to offer and, in some cases, a program of corrective training to suggest. However, at the conclusion of the interview you should allow the employee a chance to express his own thoughts on what should be done. If he has worthwhile proposals, you can probably incorporate them into the overall program, thus using participation to motivate him to improve.

14. *Follow up.* Constant follow-up is essential in a successful appraisal program. It is required to make certain the employee is

getting the training or coaching that it was decided he needed. Follow-up may be required to help the employee arrange to take any outside study courses that he may need. Follow-up allows you to check on progress and to give the employee encouragement, assistance, or even criticism when needed. Lastly, record keeping is part of your follow-up. You should have a record of your evaluation of the employee at the last interview, including remarks on how he reacted to your comments. This is helpful to you between interviews and a good bench mark that enables you to measure progress at the next appraisal session.

NINE

How to Be an Effective Subordinate

"I need Charlie Sorenson," said Henry Ford, founder of the Ford Motor Company, of his top subordinate. "He knows every operation in this business. And he sees that my decisions are carried out."

Every effective manager needs good subordinates, and this need is mutual. The relationship that you have with your superior largely determines your effectiveness as a manager in the operation for which he is responsible. You need his confidence and support, and he requires yours. Unless you share a common understanding and a common desire to achieve mutually desirable objectives, his department cannot function efficiently. His success depends on your ability to perform your assignment with initiative and intelligence.

WHAT THE BOSS WANTS FROM YOU

Have you ever considered your job from the point of view of your boss? How best can you fulfill your responsibilities in a way that is most helpful to him? Managers and executives who have been interviewed on this subject have reported an amazingly similar list of qualities which they believe are important in a good subordinate, and probably these qualities are very much like the characteristics that you yourself desire and attempt to instill in your own key men. The boss wants:

1. A *"no" man, not a "yes" man.* No manager is helped by listening to his own echo. He expects and deserves the acceptance and loyal support of his decisions once they are made. But he needs facts on which to base his plans and decisions, and he looks to you to give them to him. A subordinate does his superior no favor by uncritically agreeing with him on whatever he says. The skilled subordinate knows how to point out tactfully the weak spots in his superior's proposal and to make suggestions that improve the final plan of action.

2. *To be kept informed.* This includes any development that may interfere with the success of his group in attaining its specific objectives, that is, mistakes in planning, schedule breakdowns, and operational errors that affect job results. Give him honest, straightforward reports. Also keep him informed on the climate of employee relations—for example, hard-to-settle and recurrent grievances, or changes in employee attitudes and working habits that indicate problems are ahead. Finally, you should tell him about any decisions you have made that have caused changes or revisions in standard operations. He may have given you authorization to act independently in certain areas, but he still should be told (preferably in advance) of anything you do that affects the work or procedures of his unit.

3. *You to consult with him.* It is his job to advise you on matters that may cause you trouble. It is better to check to make sure when you are uncertain than to try to move forward on your own and run the risk of costly errors or the needless loss of time.

4. *You to report information promptly, accurately, and completely.* What to report? How soon? That is a matter of judgment.

But you will probably satisfy the most demanding boss if you follow the rule, "Late news is worse than no news," and provide the boss with a full account of the situation as you see it as soon as possible.

5. *Reports to be objective.* Do not editorialize. Give the boss the opportunity to make his own interpretation of the facts. If he wants your views, he will ask for them.

6. *Reports to be well organized.* It is important to think through what you want to say before you begin to talk. This enables you to give your superior a coherent, factual message from which irrelevant details have been eliminated. Careful preparation also permits you to give information in orderly sequence, with the stress on one main point at a time. Such a report provides your superior with a sharp picture of exactly what has happened.

7. *You to know your job.* A good manager at any level must have a solid technical understanding of his job. He must be able to get the facts needed to solve problems and know how to interpret them. He must be able to establish objectives for his subordinates and plan how to attain them. He must decide what to do when confronted with problems or emergencies. He must be able to organize work in such a way that employees are properly placed to perform the related tasks that need to be done to accomplish specific goals. He must know how to keep employees informed, how to give them instructions. He must be able to set reasonable standards of performance and provide employees with the training they need to meet those standards. He must be able to apply controls and to measure progress toward established objectives. He must be able to administer rules and policies fairly and consistently, and he must know how to adjust employee complaints and to counsel and advise subordinates on job-related problems. In short, he should be able to offer the same kind of evenhanded, objective leadership to his own subordinates that he hopes to receive from his superior.

THE ROLE OF THE SUBORDINATE

Great leaders in every human activity have always had extremely effective subordinates. Such key men are essential to a leader's success. A capable subordinate may be described as his superior's alter ego. He is by no means a blind extension of his authority, executing orders literally. But he has learned how to anticipate the boss's demands and to satisfy them before they are made. He is willing to take the risks that accompany his responsibility.

A competent supervisor has long ago learned the lesson that the authority of his superior is not a protective cloak that he can throw around himself as a shield against criticism if things go wrong. He understands that instructions must be carried out according to the circumstances of a particular situation, and he does not hesitate to modify them if that is necessary in order to achieve an objective. But to do this and still not overstep the bounds of his authority is no small act of leadership in itself.

A supervisor who considers himself a sort of human transmitter whose job ends when he tells employees what "the boss" wants them to do provides no real leadership at all. Employees realize he assumes little responsibility for results and wants only to make sure that he has carried out instructions to the letter. They regard him as a supervisory "middleman" attempting to avoid personal risk by rejecting accountability whenever possible.

A good supervisor is the floor leader of employees—their coach. To be successful every team must have a coach, someone who can appraise a situation and decide what to do. Glenn Gardiner, management adviser, once wrote, "A team without a coach rarely wins games. Authority exists in business because of the basic need of a group for leadership and direction. Good team effort rarely comes without proper exercise of authority."

Willingness to accept and properly use authority is an important factor in shaping your boss's judgment of your managerial ability. Too many supervisors and executives shy away from risks. They prefer to take what they consider the safe course and to get their superior's advice and approval on every decision.

General Lucius Clay, when he was chairman of the board of one of the major can companies, made this point, remarking, "The danger is not that too many subordinates will exceed their authority. The problem is how to get most managers to use the authority that has been given to them when they have to make one of those hard decisions that can go either way."

While it is true that a good superior does not wish his subordinates to be "yes" men, he does not consider the chronic objector of much help either. The supervisor or manager who thinks of himself as hardheaded and practical because he opposes every new idea, disregarding the benefits and looking only for the disadvantages, soon gets the reputation of being needlessly argumentative and uncooperative. At staff conferences his negative attitude compels him to argue and debate even minor details of proposed plans long after others have accepted them, and his contributions to discussions are of little value. So constant is his criticism that it soon becomes taken for granted, and even if he should offer valid reasons for opposing a particular decision, they are likely to be ignored. He has not learned to distinguish between negative opposition and constructive criticism, with the result that his opinions and views have little influence on organizational activities.

WHY CAN'T YOU GET IN TO SEE THE BOSS?

An effective manager should be accessible to his subordinates. But the extent of that accessibility often depends on the subordinate himself. Time is limited. The boss has many thing to do, and he will give more attention to assistants who relieve him of some of his problems than to the ones who create problems for him. Review your own methods and make certain that in performing your job you are giving him no reason to keep his office off limits to you.

1. *Do you reverse the process of delegation?* Do you try to solve problems yourself, or do you simply take them to the boss and ask him to give you the answers? If the latter, you are asking him to do your work. Even the best subordinates sometimes need advice and assistance, but generally they try to develop a plan for overcoming their difficulties before they see their superior. Their recommendations may need amplification or tightening up, but they have given the boss something to work with.

2. *Do you always give excuses for mistakes?* Some supervisors may be late on deadlines but always on time with alibis. According to them, it is never really their fault, whatever happens. Excuses are the refuge of the immature. Even good ones do not always protect you from blame. If a supervisor resorts to them too frequently, his legitimate excuses are discounted. The boss wants to hear that the work has been done, not the reasons why it could not be.

3. *Do you have a negative point of view?* The persistent pessimist is difficult to live with. A doleful shake of the head accompanying the words, "I don't see how it can be done," or "It simply won't work," is not the path to anybody's good side. Criticism is most helpful when it is positive and constructive. If you have sound reasons for objecting to a decision or a plan, explain them clearly and offer well-thought-out alternate proposals.

4. *Do you take your personal difficulties to your boss?* The office of your superior is not a complaint counter. Yet some supervisors persist in using it that way. The boss is asked to straighten out arguments with other supervisors, with problem employees. He is given reports on his subordinate's bad health, money worries, domestic affairs. You cannot blame the boss for trying to avoid this type of supervisor. He is not a domestic counselor, a doctor,

or a lawyer, and he does not like to be called on to arbitrate disputes between his own subordinates.

5. *Do you frequently argue with the boss?* Some people cannot keep out of arguments. They like nothing better than to debate the pros and cons of every subject. Arguing with the boss is poor judgment. His job is to direct the department, not to carry on a running debate with a subordinate on how it should be done.

6. *Do you believe others receive preferred treatment?* You may be right. But possibly it is your own fault. If you are on the constant lookout for signs that you are being discriminated against, you are likely to interpret everything your boss says or does as somehow being directed against you. Other people are promoted, you are passed over; other people get raises, your salary remains the same; you are never considered for assignments that bring recognition. These are your constant complaints. As a result the boss writes you off as a chronic griper. If you have a valid grievance, the boss should know about it. But the trouble with the constant complainer is that it soon becomes almost impossible to distinguish between his real troubles and his imaginary ones.

7. *Do you take up too much of the boss's time?* Some supervisors want to make every visit with the boss a social occasion. This is a mistake. His office is not a lounge. Tell him what you have to say briefly and clearly. If he wants you to relax and talk things over, he will let you know. Let him keep the initiative and never overstay your welcome.

8. *Do you get involved in activities of other departments?* It does not add to your prestige or influence if you are constantly involved in disputes with other departments and forced to send distress signals to your boss to give you support. The success of an organization depends on teamwork. If you expect cooperation from others, be prepared to give it yourself.

9. *Can the boss depend on you in emergencies?* A person who sidesteps responsibility in difficult assignments, or who when things go wrong depends on others to take over and straighten

matters out, may perform routine assignments satisfactorily. And that is all that he is likely to get. What is more, he will not see too much of the boss. There is little for them to talk about.

10. *Do you observe organizational lines of authority?* The most certain way to fall into your superior's bad graces is to go over his head. By doing so you may win a battle but you will probably lose the war. Would you trust a person who went over your head to attain his ends? If you do not have confidence in a subordinate, you probably have very little to say to him and are likely to be suspicious of what he tells you.

KEEPING COMMUNICATIONS MOVING UPWARD

Moving communications upward is an important responsibility of an effective subordinate. But it takes judgment to carry it out properly. What do you tell the boss? When? How? These questions trouble many managers. Here are some suggestions that may help you answer them.

1. *Give him the story straight.* Do not conceal information or play down facts. Omitting information or glossing over it for fear that its revelation might expose you to the boss's censure usually makes matters worse. Tell what happened like it happened, and if you made mistakes, admit them. After all, an error that is identified can be corrected, and the boss will probably understand. He has made mistakes himself.

2. *Do not use upward communications to oversell yourself.* If you have done a good job, let the results speak for you. It is bad judgment to blow your horn too loudly. A quick way to lose listeners is to speak long and glowingly of your own accomplishments.

3. *Do not try to protect the boss.* Some subordinates attempt to shield their superior by guarding him from people or problems which they think will needlessly intrude upon his time. He has a

right to make his own decisions. Never mistake officiousness for efficiency. Let your superior decide whom he wants to see and what problems he wants to handle personally.

4. *Do not postpone a bad report.* Bad news will not vanish. "Waiting until tomorrow" has gotten many a manager in trouble. It is always wise to consider the right moment to release any kind of information—including bad news. Moreover, if you can straighten out the difficulty before you make the report, it will be of less concern to your superior. However, a boss will be twice as angry if he has to find out what happened himself than if it is reported to him fully and frankly. He may be better able to evaluate the situation than you are because he may have information you do not. Even if he cannot totally undo the damage, it may be possible for him to reduce its effect before the results become more serious.

5. *Do not assume the boss already knows.* If you and an associate decide the boss should have certain information, make sure he gets it. Do not simply rely on your colleague to carry the message. He may be placing the same reliance on you. Agree between yourselves who will be spokesman, and if it is your colleague, check to make certain the information has been delivered.

6. *Consider timing.* Proper timing is essential. Select the right occasion. If the boss is totally occupied with a big problem, do not interrupt with a small one. Attitude and manner are also important. If you are too aggressive and interrupt your superior when he is busy, he may be so annoyed with your lack of consideration that he does not give full attention to your report. On the other hand, if you are tentative or casual in giving him information, he may not attach too much importance to it.

7. *Accept responsibility.* If you believe that an abnormal situation is developing in your department (a change in employee attitude, an unusual number of grievances or complaints revolving around a particular issue, or anything else unusual), tell your superior. The fact that you are not directly involved does not re-

lease you from the responsibility to keep your superior advised. After all, you are a member of the management team and have accepted all of its obligations.

8. *Do not make the boss dig for his facts.* Be accurate, complete, and factual. Objectivity is also important. If you force your superior into the position of conducting a cross-examination to make sure you are not editing the news to suit your purpose, he will lose confidence in your judgment and dependability. It is never sound policy to make the boss pry for answers. The facts you failed to give him may hurt him—and you.

WHAT DOES THE BOSS THINK OF YOU?

There is no better judgment than yours on how well you are doing your job. Furthermore, in all likelihood you know pretty well how you stand with your boss. In your day-to-day contacts with him and during performance appraisal interviews you probably receive straightforward verbal information on how you are doing. But you do not have to be told in so many words to form fairly accurate conclusions. He is constantly sending signals about your work, and it is an imperceptive supervisor indeed who cannot read them.

If you think "Yes" is the right answer for the majority of the following questions, there is little for you to worry about. Your boss is satisfied, even pleased, with the support you are giving him. So long as you remember that there is always room for improvement, he will undoubtedly continue to be.

■ Does your boss frequently consult with you regarding matters that affect the department?

■ Is it his usual practice to get your advice or ask for your views before he makes a decision regarding your part of the operation?

■ When difficult or emergency jobs occur, does he often assign them to you and give you a free hand in carrying out his instructions?

- Does he ever let down and talk to you on general subjects, or use you as a sounding board on which to test his ideas?
- How about salary increases? Do the raises you receive compare favorably with those of other supervisors in your department? (If you get minimum raises or are often passed over, you can be sure the boss is trying to tell you something.)
- Does your boss support your decisions and stand up for you if some decision you have made is criticized by higher management?
- Does the boss ever drop by just to exchange small talk?
- When you make a mistake, does the boss call it to your attention in a constructive way so that you can profit from the experience?

BECOMING AN EFFECTIVE SUBORDINATE

An important move you can make to increase your effectiveness as a subordinate is to step up the efficiency of your own work group. Some supervisors are fearful of taking such an initiative. Although they realize that their own and the boss's reputations depend on the results they get from the work of their subordinates, they hesitate to make suggestions or offer recommendations for improvement for fear their ideas might be at odds with those of higher management. They reason, "It is better and safer to wait and let the boss make changes when he thinks they are necessary. He might think I'm trying to do his job if I keep pushing my ideas at him."

Certainly nobody likes a know-it-all subordinate who exceeds his authority, but you will never get into difficulty with a superior if you are able to come up with solid, workable plans that improve operations. Furthermore, if you can give your boss practical ideas on how to solve various departmental problems, not only will he listen but he will begin actively to seek your advice. Regarding your own operation you are the authority and and your opinions on anything concerning it should certainly be considered by your superior when he makes decisions.

The following checklist provides recommendations that will help keep you on top of your job and able to provide your superior with the solid support he requires to stay on top of his.

1. *Be the authority on your assignment.* Closely examine and analyze every part of your activity. Prepare a list of such items as production, safety, housekeeping, scrap control, and quality and quantity control and systematically check to make certain every function meets standard. If you are completely informed on your operation, you understand which parts of it could be improved by better technology. Thorough job knowledge enables a manager to utilize new methods and machinery effectively and get the best from the talents of his people.

2. *Inventory your personnel resources.* The combined skills and talents of your employees are the tools you use to get your work done. They are your most important assets. Make sure you know such facts as the extent of the skills of your personnel, their promotion potential, and how old they are. Information of this kind permits you to keep your superior informed on your replacement requirements and to answer his questions on who is prepared for advancement, who is qualified for other types of work, and who with additional training might move into a different or newly created job.

3. *Study the structure of your organization.* Change is constant. Job changes occur as new methods and machines are introduced. If you have a fingertip knowledge of the number of skilled, semiskilled, and unskilled people in your group, you know what resources you have available to meet changing conditions and can determine whether or not present personnel can be trained to perform new jobs or if it will be necessary to recruit employees with new and different skills.

4. *Do your best to establish stability in your work force.* It is good insurance against poor employee relations. High labor turnover is also costly. If the turnover rate in your department moves sharply upward, try to pinpoint the cause. Your superior wants this information. It may be helpful in restructuring certain jobs or com-

bining them with others to make them more interesting. Also, if management knows what is causing a disproportionately high labor turnover in any part of its organization, it can formulate a more realistic recruitment program and possibly correct the situation.

5. *Sell change in advance.* Changes are disconcerting, particularly if they come abruptly or have an unfavorable effect on an employee's job or job security. Fear of the unknown affects us all. If a rumor spreads that sweeping technological innovations are coming, you can expect it to have a dampening influence on employee morale. Make it a practice to give advance announcements of coming changes and explain honestly what effect they will have on individual employees. This will minimize resistance. Often it is not too difficult to sell the benefits of change. When a job is eliminated by improved technology, your knowledge of the work force, of operations, and of the structure of your department's organization will enable you to recommend to your boss how its incumbent might be shifted to some other work. Assistance of this kind makes planning easier and gives employees a chance to adapt to new conditions.

6. *Make sure job descriptions are accurate.* There is nothing more useless than an out-of-date job description. Jobs constantly change, but all too frequently job descriptions fail to change with them. If you keep your superior advised as to how technology is altering job descriptions in your group, he can make better forecasts and you can plan future training programs with greater precision. Also, job descriptions kept up to date serve management and employees as realistic charts of their duties.

7. *Train employees carefully.* Highly trained, efficient employees assure your reputation and add to your boss's prestige. Keep informed on modern training methods. Staff experts can help with ideas on techniques and can supply visual aids and useful training material. Also, study the methods of managers who are themselves capable at training. You will pick up many new thoughts that will make your instruction more effective.

8. *Do a good job in labor relations.* Know the union agreement and how to apply its provisions. If you find that certain clauses are needlessly restrictive and a hindrance to production, explain to your boss exactly why you think they should be modified. Such facts are essential to negotiators if contract improvements are to be made at the next bargaining talks.

9. *Learn how to be a good employment interviewer.* Although applicants for various jobs in your group may have been sent by the personnel department, you have got to work with them. Make sure the people you take are qualified by attitude, experience, and skill. It is also wise to consider the applicant's potential and trainability.

10. *Represent management properly in communications.* Your example, attitude, and leadership help create the employee's image of the company. You are its agent, its spokesman. If you represent management well, up-and-down communications will be swift, effective, and natural. Employees will have a better understanding of why they are protecting their own future when they work efficiently to assure the competitive position of their organization.

11. *Establish a reputation for integrity.* Honesty underwrites a good communications program. Treat subordinates as mature men and women, and when unpleasant information must be given, do not try to disguise it with soft words or half-truths. Such an approach increases your problem.

12. *Be consistent.* Employees respect a superior who gives them evenhanded, consistent leadership. They want a manager who remains calm in emergencies, has control of his emotions, and by his own self-confidence establishes a climate of confidence in his operations. His supervision does not fluctuate according to his mood. His subordinates know what to expect and do not worry each morning about what kind of humor he is in.

TEN

How to Plan and Implement Your Own Program of Management Development

"What do you have to do to get promoted around here?" is a question that is very much on the minds of ambitious supervisors and executives.

Standard Oil of California recognized the need to give its people a specific answer and published a set of standards that it uses as a guide.

To be eligible for advancement the supervisor:

1. Gets his job well done and also on schedule
2. Knows his job and also why it's important
3. Is willing to take on all assignments given
4. Shows an ability to work well with people
5. Is able to quickly adjust to new assignments
6. Can accept criticism without any resentment
7. Is willing to accept responsibility and to learn because he's interested in doing a better job*

* *Foreman & Supervisor*, Executive Services, Inc., June 15, 1961, p. 2.

A thoughtful study of these standards is revealing in that they all either directly or implicitly require managers to continue to grow on their jobs, to continue to improve their abilities and sharpen their talents. Actually there is no other choice—that is, if you hope to maintain your competence in accepting and carrying out challenging assignments in an ever-changing industrial environment. There is an inflexible law ruling all human beings that decrees there is no such thing as standing still. You must move either forward or back. A manager who thinks, "At last I have gotten the promotion that I always wanted; now I can relax and take it easy," is starting his trip downhill and is not even aware of it.

SELF-DEVELOPMENT IS UP TO YOU

It is strictly up to you to plan your own program of self-development, one that is attuned to your own needs. Your boss or an associate whom you admire can give you helpful suggestions and advice. You can also get information and assistance from the training staff and from books and magazines. But it would be unwise to adopt unselectively anybody else's program or ideas.

Every good executive and supervisor has his own style of managing. It is based on his personality and reflects his character. Of course there have been people for whom you have worked who have exerted a profound influence on your thinking and methods. But if you imitate them too exactly, you are likely to acquire their faults, although you may benefit from their strong points. The best approach is to blend the result-getting methods of other people with your own and in that way evolve an individual style that is comfortable and peculiarly yours. The objective of a self-development program is always to strive to be yourself—your "best" self. So long as you have that attitude, you will continue to grow.

Phil Wrigley, successful industrialist and owner of the Chicago Cubs, warned against the danger of copying too faithfully the methods of a person whose accomplishments you respect.

By doing so, you needlessly impose boundaries on your ability to grow in your own right and are always so busy wondering what your model would think or do in a particular situation that you destroy your own initiative. If there are two people in an organization who think exactly alike and are always in agreement, there is no need for one of them.

Self-development is an individual responsibility. All a company can do is provide its people with the opportunity to improve their skills and enlarge their professional competence. An executive of General Electric emphasized this point when he observed,

> We provide a broad range of executive and supervisory development programs. They are intended to stimulated and challenge our management people and help them improve their abilities. But how much value a particular supervisor gets from the training we offer is strictly up to him. Any manager who wants to become a better manager must understand that his success depends almost entirely on his own motivation and continuing effort.

Self-development is a self-imposed assignment, and its final objective is beyond reach. Human perfection is a goal, never an achievement. But when a manager discontinues his attempts at self-improvement, he begins to retrogress. Complacency and self-satisfaction set in and motivation is deadened.

While there is no all-purpose plan for self-development, there are certain commonsense rules that should be followed in planning your self-development program. They are:

1. *Do not be too ambitious in your planning.* This leads to discouragement and possibly the abandonment of the program. No program will bring about an instant transformation from what you are today to what you hope to be tomorrow. Self-development is a continuous and steady process. Follow a plan that will take you to your goal step by step.

2. *Be systematic.* The day-by-day effort brings the most certain and lasting results. Self-improvement may come about so slowly that you are hardly aware of your growth. Then, all of a sudden, it happens. You find that you have eliminated weaknesses from your

performance that were holding you back, and that parts of your job that once caused you trouble no longer are a problem.

3. *Develop your own plan.* Somebody else's may not be suited to your needs or temperament. Tailor your plan to your own needs and push it ahead at your own pace so long as it is a steady one.

RATING YOURSELF

The best starting mark for a self-development program is an honest and critical evaluation of your abilities and liabilities. If you know precisely where you stand, you can plan your forward progress with greater confidence and precision. The following self-rating quiz will help you do this. Score 2 points for each question you check with a "Yes" and 1 point for "Some of the Time." The distance between the score you give yourself and 100 is a fairly accurate measure of your room for self-improvement. If you give yourself 70 points or better, you can consider yourself a good supervisor who is trying to become a better one. A grade of 95 to 100 means you are either fooling yourself or are too good to be true.

A. PLANNING   *Yes Some of the time No*

1. Is the work of your department well-planned, are possible bottlenecks foreseen and avoided, and is employee workload distributed, etc., in a way to flatten out production peaks and valleys?

2. Is your work schedule usually well planned ahead of time?

3. Do you develop sensible procedures to accomplish group objectives?

4. Do you give sufficient attention to resources needed; i.e., equipment, material, supplies, manpower?

5. Do you give careful attention to the selection of employees qualified by skill, training, experience, and judgment to do the various jobs?

B. ORGANIZING   Yes Some of the time No

6. Do you have a sound understanding of the policies, practices, and objectives of your department and company?

7. If a policy or procedure is not attaining desired results, do you inform your superior and suggest how improvements might be made?

8. Do you make a consistent effort to explain company policies, procedures, and objectives to employees?

9. Do you explain to employees how lines of authority function, and how their jobs relate to other jobs?

10. Are you keeping accurate job descriptions and doing your best to make sure they change when jobs change?

11. In instructing employees, do you say clearly how a job should be done and when completed?

12. Do you organize your work so well that only new employees need close supervision?

13. Are workloads evenly balanced, and do you make certain each employee is pulling his full weight?

14. Do you organize work in such a way that employees are busy and that idle time is at a minimum?

C. CONTROLLING

15. Do you keep production and control records accurate and up to date?

16. Do you maintain adequate records on such items as absences, tardiness, grievance settlements, discipline cases, and appraisal interview results?

17. Are your reports to your boss accurate, complete, and on time?

18. Do employees know exactly what is expected of them?

19. Do you establish standards of performance which employees understand and accept as fair and reasonable?

Yes Some of the time No

20. Do you make sure Personnel and other interested departments promptly receive information they need for permanent records?

21. Do you make frequent inspections of machines, tools, equipment, and working conditions?

22. Do you coordinate the work of your department with that of other related departments?

23. Do you work cooperatively with other departments and other supervisors and keep them informed on problems of mutual interest?

24. Do you get along with staff people and with managers who have functional authority in some areas of your operation, and do you provide them with information and data which they require to do their work?

25. Do you handle problems with other departments tactfully and strive to work out satisfactory solutions to such difficulties?

D. RELATIONSHIPS WITH SUB-ORDINATES—COMMUNICATIONS

26. Are you available to employees, and do they feel free to discuss job-related problems with you?

27. Do you encourage and credit employees for suggestions and ideas on the improvement of job methods, working conditions, housekeeping, safety, cost control, scrap reduction, etc.?

28. Do you try to provide leadership that encourages group self-discipline and makes company regulations self-enforcing?

29. Do you sell employees on the importance of their jobs and show your appreciation for their contributions to the attainment of departmental objectives?

30. Do you keep employees informed on coming job changes, new policies, policy revisions, and other matters that affect them on their jobs?

31. Do you respect and treat each employee as a mature individual who is helping you carry out your assignment?

Yes   *Some of the time*   No

32. Do you encourage upward communications, listening to employees' complaints (even imaginary ones) and problems, and helping them with advice and counsel?

E. DISCIPLINE AND GRIEVANCE HANDLING

33. In the administration of discipline are you evenhanded, fair, and consistent?

34. Are you impartial in your relationship with employees?

35. Do you make it a point to try to settle grievances promptly?

36. Do the penalties you impose show that you are familiar with the union agreement, proper procedure, precedent, and the employee's record, and are they in line with the seriousness of the offense?

37. Do you tell your superiors what parts of the union agreement need improvement or revision?

38. Are your decisions in grievance and discipline cases usually supported by top management?

F. SELECTION, TRAINING, AND APPRAISAL

39. Do you work with Personnel in the recruitment of new employees, supplying job descriptions if needed and explaining your exact needs?

40. Do you strive conscientiously to improve your interviewing methods?

41. Do you give thoughtful attention to job placement, and is your induction and orientation program well planned and thorough?

42. Do you consistently try to identify training needs, and do you seek the advice and help of the training staff to improve your methods and to develop instruction courses for the various jobs you direct?

43. Are you effective in performance appraisal interviews, keeping employees informed

Yes Some of the time No

on how they stand, what they do well, and where they need improvement, and offering assistance and instruction?

G. SELF-DEVELOPMENT

44. Are you taking any courses, attending any seminars or programs, doing any outside reading to improve your managerial ability and help keep you up to date?

45. Are you a participating member of any professional education organization or management association (for example, a supervisors' club), and do you ever take part in developing such programs?

46. During the last six months have you provided your superior with any suggestions, recommendations, or ideas as to where and how improvements could be made in operations, working conditions, policies, or rules?

47. Do you adapt well to changing conditions and work conscientiously to accomplish such transitions smoothly and with minimum disruption to people or operations?

48. Do you accept constructive criticism positively and act on it?

49. Even when you disagree with higher management on a decision, policy, or program, do you work loyally to implement it without reflecting your critical or adverse views to subordinates?

50. Do you consider yourself a member of the management team and carry out the responsibilities that have been assigned to you as conscientiously as if you were operating your own company?

A SUPERVISOR'S GUIDELINES TO PRACTICAL SELF-DEVELOPMENT

Untrained raw talent, even when combined with a capacity for natural leadership, is seldom enough to propel a person to his goals and support him there for very long. Ability and leadership must be disciplined to produce lasting results, and this requires hard work. But then, the road to achievement is usually a rough one.

When he was a young fighter, Jack Dempsey, a legendary figure in boxing, was crippled by a weak left jab. He had his manager strap his right arm to his side and for long, grueling months practiced his left against his sparring partners. When he won the World's Heavyweight Championship he was a complete fighter with a left jab that was almost as dangerous as his heavy-hitting right.

Probably without realizing it, Dempsey had based his plan of self-development on a sound management principle: study your performance, identify your abilities and deficiencies, and systematically work to improve the former and eliminate or reduce the latter. A supervisor's strong points are the foundation on which he builds his career. His faults, if not corrected, can undermine that foundation.

After you have made an honest evaluation of your strengths and weaknesses your next step is to develop a sensible program of action. In devising such a program the following guidelines may be useful.

1. *Remedy educational shortcomings.* Gaps or deficiencies may be holding you back. A college degree awarded ten years ago by no means assures that you are familiar with developments in your field if you have done nothing since to keep up to date in it. Or if you left school early, do not be afraid that you are now too far behind to catch up.

There is much you can do to repair educational deficiencies if you really want to. Is your grammar bad? Do you have difficulty finding the words you need to express your thoughts? Do you have trouble communicating? You can correct these faults through adult education courses, home study, or taking part in a public speaking program.

If you are working for a company of any size, you can greatly benefit from the management development program it conducts. Specialized in-plant seminars and conferences can be helpful. Under company tuition refund programs ambitious supervisors and executives have remedied educational shortcomings by attending night classes at nearby schools or colleges—have even won college and postgraduate degrees.

However, in programming the educational improvements aspects of your self-development program it is wise to plan at long range. It cannot be done all at once. A slow, steady pace brings you solid, cumulative results that pay off in achievement.

2. *Consult with staff training people and your boss.* These experts are ready to help. Explain to the training director and his associates what you hope to accomplish and ask for advice. They can help plan a practical program of self-development that is adjusted to your personal requirements and can be of assistance if you run into problems along the way. Your boss can make sound suggestions on what specific steps you can take to further your plan of self-improvement. He may recommend useful outside study courses and help you make arrangements to enroll in them.

3. *Be sure you have a thorough knowledge of your own job.* That is the foundation on which you build your career in management. It is necessary if you expect to plan intelligently, to organize and direct the work of your subordinates, and to follow up consistently. It determines your effectiveness in training and your skill in communications.

The best way to determine whether or not you are meeting the full requirements of your position is to study your job description. Checkmark those duties on which you concentrate and which you perform well. Study the list again! What duties are not checked? The answer tells you the areas of your assignment in which improvement is indicated. You have your starting point and can begin to shore up your weak spots.

4. *Study company operations.* Do not devote so much attention to your own work that you lose sight of its relationship with the

other activities of the company. The greater your knowledge of the functions of the entire company and how they tie in with each other, the more valuable you become to management. Do not make the mistake of some supervisors who unconsciously restrict their own growth by wearing mental blinders. Their departments are their small kingdoms, and they have little interest or concern for anything that goes on elsewhere. Ask questions. Be a good listener. When there are opportunities to hear experts discuss operations unrelated to your own work, take advantage of them. The only way you can succeed to a position of greater authority is to use your present assignment as a time of preparation.

5. *Examine your efficiency.* Use a notebook. When you hear or read of methods or equipment that might help increase your department's efficiency, make a note. The same thing goes for good ideas or programs that come to your attention. Jot down questions that you want to ask before you forget them, or reference sources that will furnish information you need.

At the end of the day, using another notebook, make a record of the jobs you handled, the problems that came up, the administrative tasks you had to perform. Include the time spent on each of these items. At set periods—about every two weeks—review the record. It will tell you how you spend your time, whether or not you are devoting too much or too little attention to your various responsibilities. A good manager gives a balanced performance.

6. *Develop your social skills.* A supervisor can have job competence, ambition, intelligence, honesty, and loyalty and still be passed over in promotions. The reason is usually that he simply lacks the ability to mix well with other people. It may be he is standoffish because he is shy and unsure of himself in social situations. He may have no small talk and be unable to discuss any subject other than his work. An abrupt, argumentative way of talking, lack of flexibility, and even poor table manners have sometimes, perhaps unfairly, denied a supervisor a job for which he was by every other standard highly qualified.

If you allow social limitations to limit your career potential, it is your own fault. You can do something about it. If your interests have been centered on your job, break out of your shell. Take an interest in current events, exchange views and opinions with associates instead of debating with them. By taking a normal part in leisure activities you can build your self-confidence and overcome self-consciousness. Good manners simply show your respect for the feelings of other people.

Social skills in themselves do not take the place of job ability, but they do provide the kind of setting for ability which displays it to the best advantage. So if you take pride in being a diamond in the rough and scoff at social skills as superficial fluff, do not be surprised if the diamond turns into a golf ball and winds up off the fairway and in the rough. If two candidates of approximately equal skills are being considered for a job, the choice is likely to go to the one with the most polish.

7. *Stay informed on what is happening in business.* Reading is the way to keep up to date on developments in business, in industry, and in your own field. To some people reading does not come easily and they avoid the printed word. Do not handicap yourself. If you are not a willing reader, set aside an hour or so each day and devote it to a systematic reading. News and business magazines and newspapers like *The Wall Street Journal* and *The National Observer* provide information on events and trends in business and the world in general. Trade journals tell you what is taking place in your own field. They report on new methods and techniques that companies are successfully using and supply you with ideas that may improve your own practices. By reading you enlarge your vocabulary, increase your effectiveness as a communicator, and expand your present knowledge.

8. *Describe your development in writing.* Draw up a simple chart indicating what you consider to be your shortcomings. Beside each fault or weakness write a brief statement on what you expect to do to correct it. Move slowly but steadily toward your goals.

After you have accomplished your primary goal, establish a new and more difficult one, and keep repeating. At periodic intervals review your chart to check progress. If you are persistent, you will be surprised at the speed of your accomplishments.

9. *Be self-disciplined.* A good manager has learned to discipline himself both emotionally and mentally. Self-discipline is absolutely essential in carrying out a plan of self-development. The program you establish for yourself must be one you can live with every day. Furthermore, it must be regularly followed. A sure way to guarantee that your efforts will end in failure is to use "on again, off again" methods. Such an approach causes discouragement and eventually the abandonment of the plan.

10. *Devise a sound method of control.* It is necessary to keep your program on the track. Have a yardstick by which you can measure your progress. A good system of controls tells you where you are, how far you have come, and whether or not you are on schedule. You require such information to correct errors in your original planning and to adjust flaws in your program when it is in operation.

THE QUALITIES OF A LEADER

No one can tell beforehand whether or not he will succeed as a leader. J. Paul Getty, the oil tycoon, has said that there are eight traits a person must have if he hopes to have a highly successful business career. Here is a summary of his list:

1. *Motivation.* You must be highly motivated and dedicated to your work. Desire to succeed will help you overcome disappointment, frustration, and setbacks.

2. *Initiative and self-reliance.* Leadership is a lonely job. The higher you climb, the lonelier it becomes. Nobody is going to do your job for you. You need self-confidence and initiative to move forward.

3. *Adaptability.* Flexibility of mind permits you to cope quickly

with unexpected changes or developments. A good leader adapts his plan to the situation as it is, not as he hoped it would be.

4. *Resilience.* You can't win them all. You are bound to have slumps and reversals. Accept them as inevitable and come on again stronger than ever.

5. *Patience.* It may take a long time to accomplish your objectives. [It took Getty twenty years to acquire Tidewater Associated Oil, and his patience was tried many times in the process.] Learn to persevere, and remember that it is fatal to try to do too much too soon.

6. *Integrity.* A good leader wins the trust of his subordinates and the confidence of his superiors. If a manager's integrity is questionable, his other attributes do him little good.

7. *Imagination, intelligence, judgment.* You must be imaginative to the extent that you can see opportunities and potential—and dangers and drawbacks. You must have the intelligence to analyze the information on which you base decisions and the good judgment to keep you from taking foolish chances.

8. *Willingness to take risks.* If you want to play it safe all the time, a career in management is not for you. Seek refuge in a job where your incumbency is protected by artificial safeguards.*

THE DEMANDS OF LEADERSHIP

Now that you have taken every possible step to improve yourself, you still must face the ultimate test imposed by the hard demands of leadership. The real answer to the question, "Can you make it as a boss?" comes in one word—character.

The methods and personalities of highly regarded leaders are never identical. A psychologist who was asked to explain what characteristics were common to them replied:

* *Chicago's American,* Sept. 16, 1961.

Who can say? They are so varied. But I have noticed that there are two things most great leaders appear to share: fear of failure and fear of sickness. These fears are closely related and lend force to a leader's drive for success. Fear of failure provides him with a tremendous will to work. Fear of sickness is due to his dread of being physically unable to do his job.

If you have those qualities that mark you as a leader, you should carefully cultivate and discipline them. Leadership is a frustrating, often discouraging responsibility. A leader must face up to hard decisions and make them regardless of personal risk. He must have the stamina to keep pushing ahead when the going is rough and must maintain the flexibility to survive setback. Above all, he must have courage and self-control. His attitudes and reactions to various situations are reflected and exaggerated by employees. If he loses his nerve in a crisis, his subordinates despair; if he is discouraged, they become despondent; if he is angry and moody, they are upset and worried.

Leadership does not automatically accompany a position in management. It must be earned by superior performance in all sorts of situations. Nor is it possible to predict with any degree of accuracy whether a person will make a good leader until he has been tested by the job. Certainly you cannot tell from appearances, for leadership comes in strange human packages.

Jacques Cousteau, famous for his deep-sea explorations, looked like an absentminded, shy, scholarly professor—an illusion that was emphasized by the amber half-lens spectacles that sat astride his nose. But Cousteau, aside from being a scientist, was an adventurer and every inch a leader. On one occasion an inexperienced diver was drowned attempting to find the anchor of his ship, *The Calypso*. The crew became unnerved and frightened. Still the anchor had to be found. Quietly Cousteau donned the dead man's aqualung and said, "I'm going down to find the anchor. Those of you who want to help, follow me." All of them went.

If you accept the responsibility of supervising other people, you have many rewards. A challenging job well done gives you a great sense of accomplishment. You have greater freedom to exercise your initiative and put your ideas into practice. There are status benefits that increase as you move upward. Finally, there is salary, which is directly related to the value of your job.

But leadership imposes a heavy burden. A manager's security depends on his job competence. His working day does not necessarily end at quitting time, and many of the decisions he must make are hard and unpleasant.

A plant manager warned a group of employees who had successfully completed a company presupervisory training course and were ready to step into supervisory jobs:

> Being a manager is not all cakes and ale. You should be absolutely certain you are mentally prepared to accept the bitter with the sweet before you decide to undertake management responsibilities. Here are some of the things that you must face.
>
> You must be ready to assume accountability for the errors of your subordinates. Sometimes the criticism that is leveled at you is unfair, but as boss you cannot shift the blame. You are still responsible.
>
> You must be able to overcome discouragement and keep trying. When a program you hoped to start is rejected or somebody else gets the job you think should have gone to you, you must learn to conceal your disappointment and try to do even better work.
>
> You must learn to keep your personal problems to yourself. Domestic or financial worries should not be allowed to affect your moods or attitudes on the job. Empoyees are entitled to consistent leadership.
>
> You must do your best even though there is no penalty for slacking off. Pride in excellent performance is the hallmark of good leaders. If the boss takes it easy he kills the incentive and destroys the morale of subordinates.
>
> You must ask yourself if you can keep your head and keep control in a crisis. Anybody can be a manager when operations are running smoothly. But when problems come and trouble mounts on trouble, employees expect you to take charge and bring things back to normal.

You must be able to take orders as well as give them. You may not agree with the boss's instructions, but if they still stand after you have given him your opinion, you should carry them out properly or get out.

You must be able to smile when recognition for your idea goes to somebody else. It is never pleasant when another person takes a bow for a program or plan that you have developed. It is even annoying if you think your boss failed to credit you properly for a suggestion or recommendation for which he received praise from his superiors. Do not let frustration or anger cause you to lose your head. If you keep coming up with ideas that work, recommendations that strengthen planning, and programs that produce results, it will not be long before you are recognized for your talents and abilities.

If you can rise to the challenge of leadership, accept the built-in risks, and are interested in the rewards of accomplishment as opposed to better pay, status, and perquisites, a stimulating career is open to you. But if you are afraid of risk, are easily discouraged, and view a job as a means to earn money for other activities, perhaps you would be wise to remain in a rank-and-file position. It is no disgrace not to want to be a leader, but if you accept the responsibility of supervision when you know you cannot provide employees with the leadership to which they are entitled, you are letting them down. Most of all, you are letting yourself down.

Index